Double Cros

Double Cross

Japanese Americans in
Black and White Chicago

Jacalyn D. Harden

University of Minnesota Press
Minneapolis
London

Published by the University of Minnesota Press
111 Third Avenue South, Suite 290
Minneapolis, MN 55401-2520
http://www.upress.umn.edu

Library of Congress Cataloging-in-Publication Data

Harden, Jacalyn D.
    Double cross : Japanese Americans in black and white Chicago / Jacalyn D. Harden.
        p.   cm.
    Includes bibliographical references and index.
    ISBN 0-8166-4043-2 (acid-free paper) — ISBN 0-8166-4044-0 (pbk. : acid-free paper)
        1. Japanese Americans—Illinois—Chicago—Social conditions. 2. African Americans—Illinois—Chicago—Social conditions.   3. African Americans—Illinois—Chicago—Relations with Asian Americans. 4. Japanese Americans—Illinois—Chicago—Ethnic identity.   5. African Americans—Illinois—Chicago—Ethnic identity.   6. Chicago (Ill.)—Race relations.   7. Chicago (Ill.)—Ethnic relations.   8. Chicago (Ill.)—Social conditions—20th century.   I. Title.
    F548.9.J3 H37   2003
    305.895'6077311—dc21   2002156539

12 11 10 09 08 07 06 05 04 03   10 9 8 7 6 5 4 3 2 1

Contents

Preface

As I prepare this book for publication, I now live in Seattle; I am no longer in Chicago. Yet during the mid- to late 1990s when I lived in Chicago, perceived by many to be the country's most segregated city, I was able to hang out with a group of Japanese American activists in their seventies and eighties. They allowed a black woman in her thirties to see that there was so much more to Asian/black history—past and present—than what is said on the streets, debated on talk radio, and written in books. Although I am no longer a part of their everyday lives, their insights and their generosity continue to help me make sense of how I read, think, and teach about race.

I could not run from the Asian/black racial politics I write about in this book even if I wanted to. Here in Seattle, which is supposed to be more racially diverse, more hip, and more livable than Chicago, lessons learned from Chicago still hold power. In August 2001 Denny Chiu of Seattle writes confidently in a letter to the editor of the *Stranger* about the real differences between Asian Americans and African Americans in that city:

> Roberts was using his vehicle to drag a police officer down the street (he caught the cop's hand in his window). The Asian American incident was *not* at all like the Central District incident. There were several dozen Asian youths instead of one lone black man; none of the Asians were engaged in violence. Maybe you don't realize that although Asians and blacks each respectively constitute about 11 percent of the greater Seattle area population, the latter account for 60 to 70 percent of violent crime here.

He compares a recent incident between Seattle police and a black man to one a month later between Seattle police and a group of Asian American students. He concludes that Asian Americans and African Americans share very little. Chiu, whose name suggests that he is Asian American, writes in coded ways about what we all secretly believe in our hearts. Asians in all their varieties are uppity and hate blacks, blacks are a culturally damaged people prone to crime who love to cause trouble, and whites are a group that more and more watches racialized battles among nonwhites from the sidelines (or, in the case of law officials, must "police" such confrontations).

After I moved to Seattle in the summer of 2000, long after my research in Chicago was completed, my husband and I traveled to the "New Berlin." I could not escape the lessons that I learned from my Chicago informants there, either. One evening we were taken to dinner at a hip and funky restaurant by two German performance artists. Both of these white women were close to my age, and I soon realized that I liked them a lot: they were politically aware and wonderfully funny and smart. During our dinner, my husband (a "good Jewish boy" from New York) and I told our hosts about our trip to the Jewish Museum earlier in the day. We both talked about Daniel Libeskind's incredible design and the power that it held for us, even without our having seen any exhibits.[1] I added how much I wished a black architect might get the chance—and the funding—to design a building for black experiences in America, and mentioned how wonderful it would be to have a building that by itself would be as moving a thought piece on black experiences in America as Libeskind's is for Jewish experiences in Germany. At this point our pleasant dinner became troubled. One of the women commented, "Of course, the museum is powerful because there is no other group in the world that has suffered as much as Jews have." She told us that she had been to the Jewish Museum and to Auschwitz. Both visits had moved her deeply. I countered that of course the Holocaust was a horrible moment in German and global history, and yes that reality was at the heart of why the museum had been so powerful, but to say that no museum could ever compare to the Jewish Museum because of the exclusivity of the Holocaust over the Middle Passage, Internment, coolie slave trade, or Europe's expansion into the New World struck me as the kind of battle royal described in Ralph Ellison's *Invisible Man* (1952). She stood firm in her conviction that the enslavement of blacks in America in no way compared to what had happened in Germany—to what her grandparents had done to Jews.

In the opening chapter of *Invisible Man*, the novel's protagonist describes an event that took place one night right after he graduated from high school. He and other young black men from the town were taken to a large hall in which the town's most important and wealthy white men gathered for fun and entertainment. The festivities included a young blond woman's striptease act, but the featured spectacle was an event that pitted the young black men against each other in one large brutal and bloody fight to the finish. Ellison makes it clear that the other participants resent the protagonist and he in turn finds them beneath him. Yet perhaps the most striking moment in the account is when the protagonist—who really just wants the powerful white men to appreciate the speech he has written, as the "smartest boy" in town, for the occasion—realizes that he and the other participants have fought and wrestled against each other in a bloody competition on an electrified mat. Instead of the pieces of gold that they had imagined, they had fought against each other for worthless junk, golden-colored automobile parts. Although Ellison's account is about the competition among young black men, today's competitions among minorities are part of an ongoing national "battle royal" in which blacks, Jews, and Japanese Americans are only three among a large and varied group of "contestants." Just as blacks and Jews seem to be competing over which group has historically suffered most, so blacks and Japanese Americans compete over the validity of reparations; now the discussions concerning reparations for slavery, both pro and con, compare blacks to Japanese Americans. In particular, the battles among people of color for the material and symbolic rewards of most favored minority, like the one Ellison describes in *Invisible Man*, pit often hostile groups against each other, while those with the "real" political and economic power sit along the sidelines watching and waiting. The levels of antagonism help to maintain the divisions among those on the mat and draw attention away from their similarities and common interests.

This book is about Japanese Americans living and working in black and white America in the twentieth century. Specifically, it is about how closely the fates of Japanese Americans have been connected to the fates of blacks in Chicago. This connection has been recrafted again and again, in part because of the danger that it poses by challenging commonly held beliefs about the nastiness and conflict among peoples of color and, in particular, between Asian Americans and African Americans. So although it is rooted in the twentieth century, this book is also about the latest installment of Asian/black dynamics in the current century. In the end I believe that what I write about here is not only about Japanese Americans in Chicago but also about all of us in Seattle, Berlin, or wherever else the color line continues to belt the world.

Acknowledgments

I owe a great deal to the Japanese American men and women who allowed me access to their thoughts and life histories. Without them this book (and I) would have gone nowhere. They never let me forget that we were on the mat together. They acknowledged the age and race differences between us. They showed me that we all could struggle to get off the mat just as much as we could struggle for the "best" position on it. It would be relatively easy for their real names to be found out, given their stature in Chicago, yet as an anthropologist I have followed my discipline's concern over using informants' real names; I have done my best to provide them with a level of anonymity appropriate for this study. I hope that their relatives and other young Japanese Americans will be able to read about them with the same amount of admiration that I have for them.

As is clear throughout this book, my relationship with my own grandmother was an important catalyst and comfort, as well as a source of consternation for how I see the world. She unfortunately did not live to see this book come to press. I often wished that she and my informants would have the opportunity to meet, but they never did. In some ways perhaps they are meeting here in this book. My grandmother and my informants all taught me much about the color line in the twentieth century, and they helped me to think about the possibilities for the twenty-first.

I must thank my parents, Charles and B. K. Harden, who have certainly wondered how they could have raised such a hardhead. All of my aunts and uncles deserve special kudos for always encouraging me to do our family proud. I must especially thank Claude Jackson Pilgrim, my Uncle Jacky. We share not only a birth date but also a name and a tenacity.

Throughout my time in graduate school at Northwestern University, I met the friends and colleagues who continue to mean so much to me. Christina Allen, Seth Cotlar, Gina Perez, Benjamin Soares, and Niels Teunis are still the first lines of defense and offense in the struggle to figure it all out. Douglas Corin, Jared Garth, and Kaylene Saddington helped to remind me how all of this started when we were living the ex-pat life in Shizuoka-ken, Japan. Northwestern faculty, including Micaela di Leonardo, Dwight Conquergood, Tim Earle, and Helen Schwartzman, deserve special mention for their advice and guidance—that taken and that disregarded.

The research here was funded in part by awards from the Consortium for Institutional Cooperation Fellowship for Minority Students and the Northwestern Alumni Association. Calls for papers for two conferences, the Hendricks Symposium at the University of Nebraska, Lincoln, in November 2000 and "Off the Grid: Urban Ethnographies and Activism," a conference at New York University in March 2001, helped me to rethink and recontextualize my research. Presenting papers at these two conferences and receiving feedback while there were extremely useful in completing this book. Students in my "Race and Ethnicity" course at Seattle University in 2000 and 2001 did not know it at the time, but their midterm essays in which I asked them to make use of drafts of two chapters of the book helped me immensely in my own rethinking of how my research might speak to the next generation of double-crossers.

Gary Okihiro and David Roediger have been terribly kind to me; their reviews of the manuscript for the University of Minnesota Press were extremely generous. They were as tough and challenging as you might expect historians reading an anthropologist "doing history" might be, yet their comments and suggestions helped tremendously. This book (and I) owe them a great deal. Carrie Mullen at the University of Minnesota Press helped this book see the light of day, and I am extremely thankful for, and in awe of, how quickly and smoothly everything progressed. Carrie "inherited" me from Jennifer Moore, the best first editor that a first-time author could ever have.

Finally, I believe that Leslie Dunlap and Steven Shaviro already know how much they mean to me. As my two best friends, neither ever complained about listening to me as I tried to get my thoughts together for the trillionth time. Words cannot be found to express how important they and their thoughts are to me and to *Double Cross*.

CHAPTER ONE

Double-Crossing the Color Line

> For the purpose of carrying out this idea [of nineteenth- and twentieth-century colonialism] the European and white American working class was practically invited to share in this new exploitation, and particularly were flattered by popular appeals to their inherent superiority to "Dagoes," "Chinks," "Japs," and "Niggers."
> —W. E. B. Du Bois, "The Negro Problems"

> Meaning is thus always multifaceted and socially contested, but it is neither absent nor unconnected with social relations.
> —David Roediger, *Wages of Whiteness*

Six years into the twentieth century, W. E. B. Du Bois predicted, "The problem of the twentieth century is the problem of the colorline" (1906: 42). Today, at the beginning of the twenty-first century, Du Bois's prediction (one of his most famous quotations) seems to have been accurate, as Americans continue to be perplexed and divided by race. Race in America exists in our minds as a series of images, past and present, of jagged lines of demarcation between blacks and whites.[1] Although we know better, the black/white color line ideology permeates our everyday life. It is played out in political campaigns, scholarly work, and mass entertainment. Yet in "The Colorline Belts the World," the source for his famous comment, Du Bois also encouraged Americans to recognize that race in the United States was not simply a matter of black versus white or of black Americans' struggles for equality. Influenced by events of his day—a "yellow" nation's victory over a "white" one in the Russo-Japanese

War and escalating levels of European and U.S. imperialism in Asia, Africa, and South America—Du Bois predicted that the political and economic shifts of the next hundred years would turn the world upside down. He believed that "the color line in civilization [would be] crossed in modern times as it was in the great past" as people of color "awoke" and competed with whites and each other for equality (43).

Du Bois suspected that the racial hierarchies of the past would be shuffled and reshuffled throughout the twentieth century. The boundaries of race would be crossed again and again. Competitors would become allies. Allies would become enemies. I follow Du Bois's lead and focus on one of these twentieth-century relationships, born out of two groups' competition for equality in the United States.[2] One of the most important, yet rarely acknowledged, relationships between two groups of color in the United States is the one between Japanese Americans and African Americans. The lines between Japanese Americans and blacks were repeatedly redrawn as both groups struggled for political and economic equality, and this relationship continues to be critical to American ideas about race, including our contemporary faith in the black/white dichotomy. Yet today, when Japanese Americans are believed by most Americans to be model minorities who are far removed from blacks, I offer an alternate picture of Japanese American identity and agency. By linking together the lives of a group of Nisei (second-generation Japanese American) activists who have lived in Chicago since World War II and archival data since the 1940s, I show how Japanese Americans' crossing of the color line, both real and imagined, has become intertwined with widely held ideas about race, culture, neighborhood, family, and activism.

Many articles and books make use of Du Bois's color line comment. I once worked in a bookstore, and I now imagine some customer or patron asking for "that new color line book"—and the bookseller or librarian offers a three-page list of titles. Despite the risk of that vision becoming reality, my focus on the color line remains strong. I believe that the problem at the beginning of the twenty-first century is the problem of double-crossing the color line.

There are at least two ways to think about what it means to double-cross. One is to betray or to trick. The other, more literal, meaning, not found in any dictionary, is to go back and forth between two positions, bringing to mind going across a bridge or railroad and eventually returning to the original spot. This work is a double-crossing because it betrays and challenges the assumptions behind the belief that everyday multiracial existence is nevertheless best thought of in terms of black and white. I present a multilayered view of a Japanese American/black color line developing over the past century and trace how this notion simultaneously challenges and supports black/white assumptions about race. This work is a double-crossing also because of what is at its ethnographic core. It double-crosses the color line in the literal sense of the term. The professional and personal relationship that developed between me, a young black American woman researcher, and a core group of Chicago Nisei community activists in their seventies and eighties crossed gender, class, age, and racial boundaries that tend to replicate themselves in academic research. As a new century has arrived and "multiculturalism" has become both a way to essentialize identities and a way to sell anything to anybody, my research presents a case for challenging the easily accepted boundaries of identity and materiality that divide along predictable lines and divert attention away from shared existences.

This book has five chapters. Each chapter, including this introduction and the afterword, reworks the usual ways of thinking about race by concentrating on the historical and ethnographic evidence that points time and again to the importance of Japanese Americans in the development of—and challenges to—contemporary racial ideology. Chapters 2 and 3 detail both the historical and contemporary realities of the Japanese American/black relationship. Chapters 4 and 5 form the more traditional ethnographic core of the book. Through oral history and participant observation, I write about Japanese American lives that have long been interwoven with blacks and dependent upon the power of—and challenges to—the black/white dichotomy. In the afterword I argue that we must believe what may seem to be contradictions of unbelievable magnitude if we are ever to think and act beyond black and white. Between chapters, entries from my field notes and direct quotes from transcripts of interviews act as segues. They represent what is seldom seen in finished ethnographic research, but what I feel is an honesty that needs to be part of a project of this nature. These entries are not filler between chapters, but represent the ways that raw data is reworked into a finished project. Taken together, the components of the book build upon a variety of methods and theoretical perspectives to expand traditional (as well as more recently instituted) notions of what constitutes anthropological research, Asian American studies, Chicago race politics, and, most important, the black/white color line.

Although I will be discussing various moments in U.S. history from the early 1890s onward, the ethnographic present throughout this book is the late 1990s. To those who live in Chicago today, what I describe may not seem to jibe with their understandings of neighborhood boundaries and who lives within them today. The Chicago that my informants and I comment on and go about our business in is a city that will be both familiar and strange to the reader. The transformation of certain neighborhoods, from straight to gay or from working poor to wealthy, noted in this book has already taken place by the early 2000s. Some readers may not know what this or that neighborhood was like five or ten years ago. There are a series of snapshots in this book of particular moments in the ongoing process of "neighborhood transition" in late 1990s Chicago. During that time all of Chicago was undergoing tremendous gentrification, courtesy of both regional and national boom economies—particular political and economic conditions that have now passed away. In the time period that forms the backdrop of this book, the Chicago Housing Authority's Cabrini-Green buildings are still standing. The explosion of national retailers and upscale boutique restaurants (an indicator for many of the economic health of any given neighborhood in any given city) on the near north and far north sides of Chicago is still relatively new. The bulldozers have begun to make way and cranes have begun to swing for the "mixed use" and "mixed income" developments that are supposed to be at the heart of the new Chicago neighborhood. Boomtown Chicagoans are in the full swing of "rediscovering" and "rehabbing" neighborhoods that have been left to the poor and immigrants for decades. The money is flowing for real estate development, but many not-so-wealthy people, both new and not-so-new residents of the neighborhoods in transition, are angry, frightened, and resigned to the changes that will inevitably push them out and away from their current neighborhoods.

Also at the end of the twentieth century, during the bulk of my research, racial tensions among nonwhite groups in the United States, and in particular between Asian Americans and African Americans, are being played out on city streets and in op-ed pieces. Boycotts and beatings, reparations movements and anti-immigrant initiatives are the actions that stand out in contrast to the buzzwords of the decade, "multicultural-

ism" and "diversity." As Du Bois predicted, people of color are still competing with each other and with whites for political and economic equality. And race in America is still about where you fall or think you should
fall along the color line.

Race in Chicago/Race in America

In order to understand race in Chicago, so important to the term "race
in America," we have to acknowledge that it is made up of both symbol
and reality. To many, this may seem obvious. If you really pressed "a
Chicagoan," he or she would admit that there have always been more
than blacks or whites in the city (maybe even admitting that there are
different kinds of whites). All anyone has to do is think about who they
buy from, work for, or see when they walk down the street. All would
agree that Mexicans, Koreans, and Indians are as much a part of Chicago
as the black and white residents. But these same Chicagoans would probably conclude, and almost rightly so, that race in Chicago is best understood by paying attention to what happened to blacks. "Race" defined as
a black thing is a mixture of truth (the Civil Rights movement wasn't
for nothing) and fiction (no need to pay attention to Japanese Americans). But race in Chicago means more than thinking about your neigh-
bor's or coworker's color. It is much more than that. At its core the term
implies that there are reasons why race and economics in Chicago exist
the way they do today. It is a kind of code that resonates throughout the
country, from "New Democrats" to "Old Republicans." Both the creators
and the followers of these cultural beliefs push Native Americans, Latinos,
Asians, and poor rural whites aside to insist that blacks not only define
race in America best, but are the reason why race and economics are
still problems in America.[3] Many on the left, who are admittedly more
concerned about the inequalities that U.S. racism has wrought, offer up
race in Chicago as an example and justification for the continued fusion
of race and racism with African Americans, despite American histories
and experiences. For too long these views have distracted us from the
reality of multiracial life in postwar Chicago and America. The term
"race in Chicago" has made us lazy. We accept what it insists. It is easier
to blame blacks or even with good intentions make them the center of
our race theories because it is much simpler than trying to figure out
how and why we continue to do so. We do not seem to care that the tensions that go along with life in a multiracial Chicago are plentiful and

that they interfere with our images of a black-and-white city. It seems easier somehow to ignore Chicago's recent past. We can deny that multiracial/multiclass daily interactions threatened to topple the black/white color line in Chicago right after World War II. We turn away from the more unsettling questions that such contradictions raise. We do not ask or even recognize the significance of the fact that Chicagoans had to be told to accept the idea that Japanese Americans were not really "colored" and that their culture explained why it was so.

Over the past ten years Asian Americanists have paid increasing attention to Asian American/black American relations; however, this has been limited primarily to the highly publicized confrontations between Koreans and blacks in Los Angeles and New York. These researchers pay various levels of attention to the conflicts that have come out of Korean merchant/black customer relationships in urban areas. They link these points of contact to larger patterns of immigration, race, and class in the United States. Park (1996) points out that blacks, Koreans, and whites all apply some notion of cultural differences to what occurred in Los Angeles in 1991. Park calls this a "use and abuse" of the notion of culture in America and turns attention away from the economic realities behind the tensions—as well as the way that whites are able to escape blame in such models. Min (1996) centers his research in the ethnic middleman theories that have been popular with some scholars since their inception in the late 1960s. The ethnic middleman theory has most often been used to explain what appeared to many to be an undeniable truth in U.S. history. "Near white" ethnic groups—for example Jews, Arabs, and Asians—could come to the United States as merchants and eventually work their way up and out to the middle-class American dream. Min concludes that Korean relationships with blacks in inner cities are a recent addition to the long history of merchant immigrant middlemen in U.S. cities. Korean Americans are "caught in the middle" between powerful whites and poor blacks. While research like this is important, it is by no means definitive of Asian American/black American relationships.[4]

There is a need in Asian American studies to expand beyond Korean American/black American conflict. Not only because of the diversity of Asian American communities—for example, the sizable Hmong communities in Minneapolis live in close contact with large black and Native American communities—but also because not all Asian Americans are merchants nor are they all recent immigrants. We must remember that Asian American/black history did not begin in Los Angeles in 1991.[5]

When thinking about how people understand the way race works in America, it has been a double cross for sure. This has been especially true when thinking about Asians and blacks. We have been told by scholars and race leaders to see the realities of race and class discrimination through a cracked lens. Today the image that is reflected back tells only half the story. But it was not always this way. Throughout the United States people of color and whites have shared histories that confound many of our deepest thoughts about the way race works. This is not limited to Japanese Americans and African Americans or to Chicago. Japanese Americans' migration to Chicago, their relationships with blacks in particular, is just one part of the other half of the story.

In the years right after World War II, the early years of Japanese American history in Chicago, researchers and a variety of ordinary Chicagoans recognized that Japanese Americans were important to the term "race in Chicago." Then as now, Japanese Americans walked a thin line between black and white. Researchers documented Japanese Americans' tenuous positions, as well as how varied Japanese American opinions were about living and working in Chicago.

The first two decades of Japanese American history in Chicago, the 1940s and 1950s, were filled with the contradictions and uncertainties of how Japanese Americans would fit into a black-and-white city. As I will discuss in greater detail later, in order for race to become and remain a "black only thing," all Chicagoans, including Japanese Americans themselves, had to be convinced that Japanese Americans were not colored. They had to cross the color line. Crossing the color line not only meant not being associated with blacks and possibly other nonwhites, but also not being considered a problem. In such an environment, Chicago's Japanese American relocatees were used by Chicago School of Sociology researchers intent on proving that culture was at the root of different races "making it." The researchers left us with accounts of unionizers and business owners using nonwhite, but highly skilled, Japanese Americans in their struggles over power in the workplace. Their studies go beyond what they may have intended to do. Instead of supporting University of Chicago Department of Sociology (UCDS) theories of culture and assimilation, the three graduate students, themselves Japanese Americans, disrupted much of what we understood about race relations.[6] It is clear that their research subjects held a variety of opinions about what it meant to be Japanese American in postwar black-and-white Chicago. Today it should be obvious, although many still cling to culture-based explanations, that culture was not the reason Japanese Americans were "making it." There were other reasons that had a lot to do with our contemporary ideas about "Chicago as race city" and the telltale factor of "race culture" both gaining momentum from the effects of the relocation in Chicago.

Through the definitions of Japanese Americans' proper place in Chicago that began to appear during the 1940s and 1950s, the theoretical, economic, and political framework behind model minority mythology was born.[7] Japanese Americans in black-and-white Chicago came to be defined as the opposite of blacks in black-and-white Chicago, although neither group was white. "Traditional" Japanese American culture, which stood in contrast to black cultural traditions, was the reason Japanese were so different. The logic behind these images is the core of the double-cross in our contemporary ideas about race in America. Japanese Americans became the "colored" ideal workers and neighbors in Chicago. The key word is "became," because, as the Japanese American students' work demonstrates, the symbols and the realities of race in Chicago clashed in numerous ways. The disconnect that resulted from trying to fit Japanese Americans into Chicago's existing race structure helped to set the stage for the continued importance of the Japanese American role in definitions of race in Chicago—and by default, of race in America. Japanese Americans came to Chicago during the twenty years after World War II in record numbers. Although these numbers are debated among Asian Americanist scholars, U.S. census data make it clear that the impact of Japanese Americans on Chicago's racial hierarchies was significant (see Figure 1).

There are reasons, not all of which are known or can be explained, that Japanese Americans in Chicago were allowed to cross the color line. The early history of Japanese Americans in Chicago can tell us the parts of the story that show it was not inevitable, natural, or true that Japanese Americans left race behind. The presence of Japanese Americans in postwar Chicago turned race in the raced city upside down. Their relocation and our misreading of it today is one of the most influential, but overlooked, factors behind what we mean when we say "race" in America.

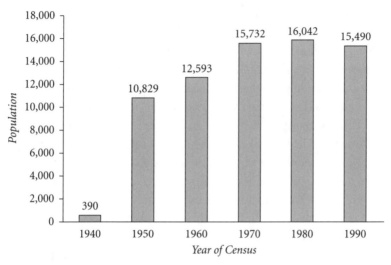

Figure 1. Number of people of Japanese American ancestry in Chicago metropolitan area, 1940–90. Source: U.S. Census.

To Be Japanese

To "be Japanese" in the United States continues be an integral part of a history of national and international conceptions of family, race, nation, political economies, and personal struggles. Over the past century Japanese American realities have been uniquely tied to the workings of race, politics, and economics in this country and, most important, to the way racial hierarchies have played themselves out. Inevitably they appeared in raced and gendered popularized images. The images of Japanese Americans may have changed over the last one hundred years, but the importance of "being Japanese" in the United States has never lost its power.[8] Early constructions in the late nineteenth and early twentieth centuries of what it meant to be Japanese to those who were not Japanese influenced the meanings of "Japaneseness" for the earliest Japanese immigrants. Whether from the mouths of public officials, the legal owners of the land that Japanese Americans worked, the Mexican workers who picked Japanese crops, or their fellow Japanese neighbors, the images of what it meant to be Japanese in America were connected to where you felt you stood in relation to immigrants from Japan. On the West Coast, Japanese Americans were part of a political economy that—more often than not—structured their already existing notions of the world and what it meant to "be Japanese." They were challenged to succeed in complicated murmurs, shouts, and proclamations of survival in an economy that was in many ways out of their control.

The world that the Issei (first-generation Japanese Americans) found themselves in was already charged with notions of raced labor and citizenship before they arrived. They came to the U.S. West Coast not only as individuals but as citizens of a nation that was attempting, courtesy of emigrants' remittances, to modernize under the scrutiny of Europe and America. The Issei, like other immigrants past and present, lived in a political economy that was structured by racial constructions, nationalistic debates, and economic realities that had direct impact on their daily lives—in both the long and short term. But then so did the U.S. citizens of various ethnicities with whom early Japanese immigrants and their families shared physical space.

For example, in 1922 the attorney general of California wrote:

> The American family reared along the lines of American traditions with the father managing the farm, the mother presiding in the home, and the children during their younger years attending school, cannot compete with the Oriental farm life wherein children and mother join with the father in the actual farm labor, and in addition do not enjoy conditions of life which are demanded by the American standard of living. (Cited in O'Brien and Fugita 1991: 23)

Thus to "be Japanese" in California in 1922 was rooted in efforts put forth by powerful white Californians to prove that Japanese Californians posed a serious threat to American "culture" and white families.[9]

Almost twenty-five years later what it meant to be Japanese had changed. Postwar images of Japanese Americans were undeniably tied to Japanese Americans' recent internment. Not surprisingly, just as whites used Japanese Americans to think about their proper place in California before the war, blacks did so after the war. To be Japanese American in Los Angeles in 1946 meant being part of a special relationship between black and Japanese Americans. *Ebony* magazine ran an article, "Of Jive and Japanese," in which the young magazine, dedicated to showing the world middle-class blacks' mettle, compared the returning Japanese American (Nikkei) families to their black American counterparts living in Los Angeles' Little Tokyo. And just as being Japanese, in the attorney general's eyes, underscored family, so did *Ebony*'s view. There seemed to be no better way to stress the similarities between the two "cultures" than to use the sexually charged imagery of a cross-cultural wedding between recently freed Japanese Americans and the black Americans who had benefited from the World War II American economy. The pre- and postwar histories of "being Japanese in America" hold power for both whites and blacks, but what about Japanese Americans themselves?

What does it mean to be Japanese in America as seen through Japanese American eyes? How does the black/white color line look from Japanese American perspectives? How is the question of the century—race in America—formulated through Japanese American lenses? The answers to these questions are few because all too often scholars and the American public accept the premise that Japanese Americans have rarely paid attention to race. Japanese American experience is seen primarily through the lens of internment and America's (white America's) discrimination against Japanese Americans. This is important, but it limits what we can learn from Japanese American history. And if there is any outright mention of race and Japanese Americans today, the tendency is to focus on Japanese American/white interracial relationships and marriages.

So there are at least three ways to think about what it has meant to be Japanese in America in terms of racial ideology. However, all three— through the eyes of whites, blacks, and Japanese Americans themselves— are intertwined within a history that reflects the country's political and economic struggles. Just as West Coast economies and histories played a crucial role in producing the existence of what is identified as the seat of Asian American culture, so did Chicago's economy and history play a part in the creation of a less-studied Asian American Chicago. Within this Asian American history of Chicago, the meanings attached to "being Japanese" in the twentieth century cannot be denied.

Japanese Americans' place in Chicago—and how the city's residents learned to think about it—has hinged upon the importance of the Japanese American/black connection in a century and a half of U.S. racial politics. And more recently, in the latter half of the twentieth century, Japanese nationals' experiences in the Chicago metropolitan area called into question how suburban cities would deal with race and class, when some of those who were "of color" were also the ones who had more money. To be Japanese in Chicago throughout the past century, whether as Japanese national or as Japanese American, meant being part of the city's role in national ideologies about families as signifiers of culture, about good versus bad neighborhoods, and about black/white relations as the center of U.S. race issues. Each of these important tropes must be reworked to understand how Chicago as a city and as a national icon has shaped the multiple meanings of "Japaneseness." Today meanings of "Japanese" and "Japanese American" in the Chicago metropolitan area are tied to contemporary local political economies and identities, just as much as they are connected with events that have taken place nationally and internationally over the past one hundred years.

Right now what it means to be Japanese in Chicago depends on the people you talk to and where they live in the metropolitan area. Black children who play in the Japanese gardens in the Jackson Park neighborhood on Chicago's South Side—what many Chicagoans surely see as one of the city's most economically and culturally challenged areas—do not know or probably even care that the city of Osaka recently funded the refurbished pavilion and gardens originally built in 1893 for the Columbian Exposition. Nor do they know about a highly charged debate about the merits of the project that took place between Japanese government officials and the city of Chicago. City officials did their best, unsuccessfully, to convince the Japanese backers that their money would be better spent in an area in which their efforts would be appreciated. But then the playing children's parents, aunts, uncles, cousins, and neighbors probably do not know that in the 1920s and 1930s black congregations in Chicago looked to the Japanese as proof that "coloreds" could show whites that the colored races were strong and powerful. And when the Kanto earthquake, one of Japan's largest and most devastating earthquakes, left much of Japan in ruins in 1923, Chicago's black congregations sent hundreds of dollars to the earthquake victims.

But these are not the memories found on Chicago's South Side. Instead the meanings of Japaneseness for many blacks have become fragments of the widely publicized derogatory statements of Japanese prime ministers that came out in the 1980s and 1990s about blacks and other people of color in the United States. For many blacks, recent memories of "the Japanese" blend with quotidian interactions with other "racist" Asians. Thus on the South Side of Chicago "the Koreans"—immigrants who run businesses in many of Chicago's predominately black neighborhoods—and "commonsense" knowledge inspired by media reports about incidents between blacks and "Asians" on both the East and West Coasts blur together. Within all of this, the ideas that Japanese Americans are not distinct from Japanese nationals and have no connection with black lives whatsoever go uncontested. Experiences gleaned from both popular culture and everyday life continue to be the principal sources of the meaning of "Japanese" for every person who lives in Chicago, regardless of the color of his or her skin.

Why Chicago?

Chicago, though not directly a seat for early Japanese immigration, is as important to consider as the West Coast when we grapple with issues of Asian experiences in the United States. As Sumida (1998) has pointed out, the traditional focus on California and the West Coast in both Asian American scholarship and the formation of Asian American identity has created "false master narratives." Because of Chicago's location outside of the West Coast, the answer to "Why Chicago?" is an easy one. The Columbian Exposition held in Chicago in 1893 was Japan's first real appearance at a world's exposition, but in addition the spectacle served as one of the first times when the meanings of "Japanese" were embodied in individual activities and observations. So as both literature—official and unofficial—and exhibits dealt with nascent capitalist-influenced global politics and economies, individual Japanese and American citizens physically connected local, national, and international politics by their actions.[10] Moreover, just as the Japanese exhibits at the Exposition were in part an allowance by officials and local "supporters" of the fair (department store magnate Marshall Field and International Harvester founder Cyrus McCormick) to the Japanese government to outshine the "heathenish and vile" Chinese, the Japanese pavilions and material goods served as contrast to Native Americans being paraded and displayed in the fair, as well as the "public Negroes" (Frederick Douglass and Ida B. Wells) boycotting the fair—literally and figuratively—outside of the fair's boundaries. But these are not just interesting fun facts to be placed into a cultural-economic stew; these events were clearly tied to the Chinese Exclusion Act of 1882 and to newly freed blacks' changing positions in the United States. These early images of Japan as "model minority" speak to the national and international politics in which the Exposition was firmly entrenched. They also lay bare the key role of Chicago, which soon began to be known as "The Midway Metropolis" after the highly successful exposition, in the production of what it meant to be Japanese in America from the beginning. The fact that this site was more than two thousand miles away from the West Coast, thought to be the locus of Japanese American identity, addresses a necessary paradigmatic shift for both Asian American studies and Chicago social history. Chicago's growth from onion field to major global city over the past one hundred years serves as a backdrop for understanding how Japanese American identities were created and maintained. Thus what it means to be Japanese in Chicago today interlocks and overlaps with a likewise constructed "Chicago."

In 1893 Chicago, a few laborers were sent from Japan by their government to build the garden and wooded isle pavilion for the Exposition. Before then there had been no real Japanese presence in Chicago. Today Japanese nationals living in Chicago are urged by their government and their employers to become more *kokusaika na* (internationalized), so once again Japanese citizens are encouraged to live and work in Chicago on behalf of their government's desires. But to be Japanese in Chicago at the beginning of the twenty-first century also means to be a Nisei, Sansei, or Yonsei (second-, third-, or fourth-generation Japanese American). Yet for many of these individuals, their very existence in Chicago is a direct result of the federal government's urgings to relocate after Japanese American Internment during World War II. And as Japanese Americans made their way into the country's most "racially segregated city," Chicago's perceived and real existence once again played a crucial role in creating the notion of a Japanese community in the metropolitan area.

There has never been a designated "Japantown" in Chicago. Today the closest thing to a Japanese neighborhood is a few clusters of businesses and social service agencies—remnants of the years right after the war when Japanese relocatees were advised to spread out in the city and keep low profiles. On Chicago's Far North Side, the patrons and owners of Latino markets and taquerias share space with the shops, churches, and cultural-retirement centers of Japanese Americans. A few doors down from the large Japanese American cultural center, a new variation on the theme of "Jive and Japanese" exists. A two-block cluster of Korean "wholesalers" draws crowds of black and Latino shoppers from the surrounding neighborhoods on weekends.

Reading the city's tourism literature, any visitor knows instantly that the city's leaders see the city as a "City of Neighborhoods." Every summer, as in many other U.S. cities, Chicago has a series of neighborhood festivals. Of course it is understood that each neighborhood festival will have its own flavor, courtesy of whatever particular ethnic group is sup-

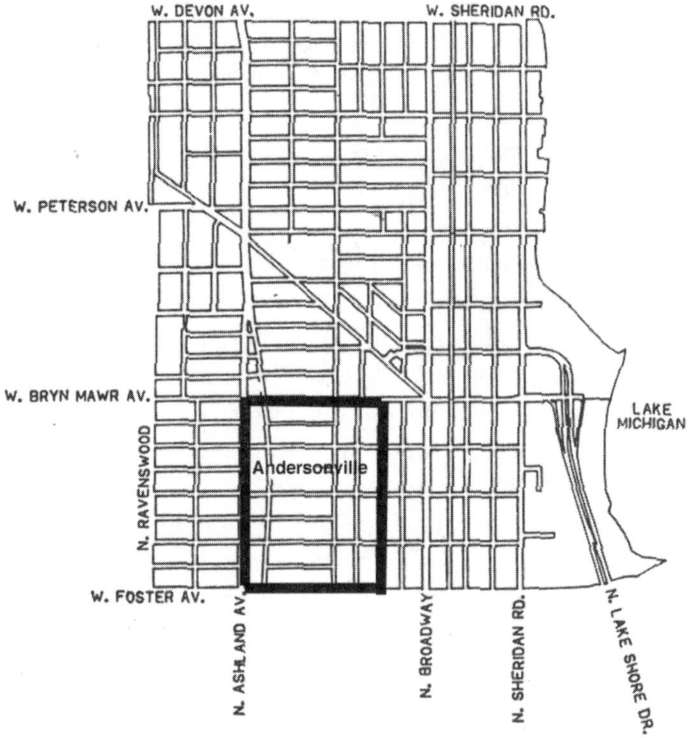

Map 1. The Edgewater neighborhood on Chicago's Far North Side. Andersonville is outlined in black. Reprinted from *Social and Economic Characters of Chicago's Population* (Department of Planning and Development, City of Chicago, 1992).

posed to live in that given geographical area. But often there is a disjunction between what the neighborhood is supposed to be and who actually lives there. With no official Japantown in Chicago, why Chicago? The answer is found in Andersonville.

The Andersonville neighborhood (see Map 1) and its Midsommarfest are examples of this. Andersonville's Chamber of Commerce defines Andersonville as bounded by Rosehill Drive (5800N), Winnemac (5000N), Glenwood (1400W), and Damen Avenue (2000W). The organization's informational booklet, "A Walk through Andersonville" (1996), tells the story of how Andersonville was named in 1850 for John Anderson, a Swedish farmer and landholder, and says that the neighborhood is home to Chicago's Swedish American Museum. Every summer, usually in June, the chamber sponsors one of the earliest of Chicago's ethnic festivals, Midsommarfest. Every year the festival planners close down Clark Street, one of Chicago's major north-south roadways, from Foster Avenue to Bryn Mawr. Vendors begin arriving early in the morning on Saturday. The site stretches for six blocks, with a stage at each end, so there is plenty for everyone to do. They set up their booths, prepare their foods, and get their informational materials ready for the huge crowds that attend one of the North Side's most popular festivals.

When you go to Midsommarfest your fellow festivalgoers are a testament to Chicago's diversity. Chicago's heat is usually in full swing, so babies, grandmothers, straights, gays, couples, singles, and large families in just about every ethnicity, race, and class combination all seem to show up for the festival—in whatever combination of sheerest and coolest clothing their personal modesty can tolerate. Police officers from the nearby Foster station come out in full force to get some sun and fill up on the food, while making sure that nobody has too much fun. There are plenty of corn dogs, cotton candy, and various local restaurant specialties for the officers and any other festivalgoers with money to sample. There are also the characteristic games of chance on which to try your luck. But after walking up and down Clark and sampling the food and merchandise for sale, it is easy to forget that this is supposed to be a Swedish American festival. Plenty of shish kebab and hummus, but no lutefisk in sight. There are lots of gay pride rainbow goods, but very few "traditional" Swedish crafts. Just as this realization hits, several blond girls run by in costume, jump on one of the stages, and with relatives grinning all the while, perform a traditional Swedish dance. And if you get out of the street and walk along the sidewalks, you begin to see that there are indeed the things you would expect from a Swedish neighborhood. The Swedish Bakery, Wikstrom's Gourmet Foods, Ann Sather's, and Svea confirm a suspicion that Scandinavian food can be found in Andersonville. The Landmark of Andersonville, a series of small shops, sits on a corner. Peering into its windows you can see small wooden carvings and the kind of small trinkets that you imagine a grandmother who still remembered the old country would want. The dried flowers, cross-stitched pillows, Scandinavian soaps, and bath salts all reassure you that this is indeed what should be found in Andersonville.

But there is still an undeniable strangeness to the mixture of other shops along Clark Street. There is a lesbian-feminist bookstore and shop after shop specializing in Turkish and Middle Eastern foods. Okee-

Chee's Wild Horse Gallery advertises itself as "Andersonville's showcase of American Indian Art." Calo's, a dark wood-paneled Italian restaurant rumored to have been the scene of a Mob hit in the 1950s, is just down the street from the Philadelphia Church, with its giant neon "Jesus Saves" sign. Across from the church is the Machu Picchu, specializing in an Andean smorgasbord. Even the mixture itself seems a study in contradiction and contrast. And if you keep walking north on Clark, still amazed at the contrast between the festival's theme and what can be purchased while attending it, you will pass the Japanese American Citizen's League (JACL) offices.

The office is sandwiched between Kang Tai, a shop specializing in Chinese and herbal medicine, and Café Ashie, a Middle Eastern restaurant specializing in "the best Mediterranean food." Café Ashie's awning advertises in big red letters, "LIVE ENTERTAINMENT." If that catches your attention and you want to know exactly what the entertainment is, there are signs in the window to let you know that Café Ashie employs a live belly dancer on Fridays, Saturdays, and Sundays. The JACL headquarters has been at that location in Andersonville since the 1970s. The organization owns the building outright and thus has one of the few Japanese tiled roofs in Chicago. There, among the eclectic hubbub of a very busy street during one of the largest "ethnic" festivals in the city, is the building where the JACL Human Rights Committee (HRC) meets once a month. If you are lucky you might catch the group of Nisei men and women who have lived in or around Andersonville for most of their postwar lives and who unselfishly allowed me into their lives in order to learn why Chicago is important in understanding what it means to be Japanese American in America.

The construction of Chicago—in concept and in reality—has taken place in conjunction with, and not separate from, the individuals who live within its borders. It is a crucial necessity to connect the development of the city's transportation system, its labor history, the development of high-rise housing projects in the south of the city as contrasted to gentrification of North Side areas, and the continuous banter about Chicago as a city of neighborhoods to Japanese nationals' concerns about their children being teased in suburban schools or Japanese Americans clinging to certain areas in the city as sites of Japanese American culture even after "moving up and out." Chicago's past and present existence as a

Figure 2. The JACL building in Andersonville.

U.S. metropolis is part of a publicly forgotten past when government officials worried about what might happen if the "Japs and the Negroes" got together.

Why Anthropology?

At the beginning of the twenty-first century the discipline of anthropology sits at a crossroads of sorts. Anthropology's trademark four fields seem to be at odds with one another. In this historical present a general reduction in funds available to researchers and theoretical differences within academic departments have caused both small- and large-scale restructuring of many departments and much discussion within the American Anthropological Association. To make matters worse, it seems to some as if what anthropology is best known for—cultural, biological, linguistic, and archaeological study of humans—is now done as well, if not better, by other disciplines. So the question to many both inside and outside the field has become "Why anthropology?" For an answer, it is helpful to understand how anthropologists are thinking about race today. There has been a trend over the past few years to examine anthropology's role in U.S. race theory and politics—often with contradictory conclusions and approaches.

Figure 3. Looking north on Clark Street in Andersonville.

Anthropologists, who research what it means to be human, under-standably have long been interested in the questions surrounding race's cultural and biological meanings. There has been a resurgence of interest among anthropologists in the discipline's intellectual history with regard to race.[11] This renewed interest in anthropology, race, and culture has pointed out that anthropology's historic role after World War II in classi-fying "race" as an inappropriate term for thinking about human differ-ence was a key turning point in anthropology's exclusion from the "van-guard when it comes to debates on race, racism, multi-culturalism, or revising the canon" (Visweswaran 1998: 70). Well-intentioned efforts by cultural anthropologists in the 1950s to replace "race" with "ethnic group" and to use "culture" instead of "race" helped to make *R* a kind of scarlet letter among anthropologists. The result has been that anthropology, in an effort to combat the scientific-based racism that it helped to create at the turn of the last century, has tended to ignore the social, political, and economic realities of race in the United States in particular. Today the term "race" has become an unfavorable or risky term among an-thropologists, who instead research and write about culture and ethnic groups. It has been suggested that anthropology's move helped to nurture a climate in which the culture wars of the 1980s and 1990s flourished.[12] Given these developments, there are calls for anthropology and its practitioners to pay closer attention to the historical and cultural contextualizations of race and to the place of such constructions in everyday life. This "new study of anthropology and race" not only calls for an examination of anthropology's role in the historic race-culture-racism dynamic, but also stresses the continued importance of anthropological theories and methods in U.S. race theory and debates.[13]

Race is indeed a socially constructed reality with a power and a weakness that comes from the contradictions that surround it and us. My belief that living within such contradictions is part of what it means to be human fuels these fundamental questions. First, where do Japanese Americans fit within past and present notions of race and divisions of color in the United States and abroad? Second, did Chicago's political economy and its image as the typical "black and white city" have anything to do with Japanese American lives in the twentieth century? Third, what happens when Japanese Americans are put into the spotlight instead of blacks, when we ask about the contradictions of race, and how does this speak to the way in which "the color line belts the world"? And fourth, could the Japanese American/black connection be so well hidden, ignored, and denied exactly because it is a fundamental component of how "race" in America works?

Why Japanese American/Black Race Politics?

It isn't just what it looks like, but what it feels like. This is what yoga teachers tell the beginners. As in yoga, the "politics and economics of race" is as much about image as it is about the realities that define it. In the rest of this chapter, I want to discuss why I have grounded my work in what I call Japanese American/black race politics theory. Japanese American/black race politics theory argues that the relationships between Japanese Americans and blacks throughout the twentieth century, real and imagined, historically posed a threat to hegemonic notions about the importance of a black/white color line. Although I am trained as an anthropologist, my approach is methodologically adventurous as it flows back and forth among three different schools of race theory—anthropology, history, and cultural studies—to offer an alternative to what I have experienced as antagonistic circling of disciplinary wagons. Throughout my relatively short career in academia, I have learned that there are as many rewards as there are dangers in doing "interdisciplinary work." Japanese American/black racial politics theory demands such an approach.

In the chapters that follow I pay attention to media images of Japanese Americans as they have offered different audiences different configurations of the Japanese American/black relationship. I also examine how at specific moments in U.S. history, these pictures and words helped to create today's images of Japanese Americans as the country's most powerful economic minority and black Americans as the country's most successful political minority. At the same time I also offer testimony from Japanese Americans who have "lived" the images and argue that this division of power has tended to diminish any possibility that the two groups would ever join forces in protest.

The two components of Japanese American/black race politics theory—how racial identity and ideology are connected to shifts in economics and politics at particular moments in history and how both the images and realities of Japanese Americans and blacks center around nationwide arguments about work and civil rights for minorities—reveal why Japanese American and black relationships have always had the power to upset the ways that Americans think about work and political power in the United States.

Portrayed in a wide variety of outlets as competitors in a race to become America's favorite minority group, Japanese Americans and blacks really have competed for jobs and respectability. Japanese American/black race politics as a construction, inter alia, has served to make the dynamic between "Japs" and "Niggers" as important to the continuation of economic and political inequality in the United States as the more familiar ones between whites and nonwhites.[14] These conditions have kept Japanese Americans and blacks—not to mention the American public—from recognizing and protesting shared situations of economic and political discrimination throughout the twentieth century. Yet where Japanese American/black race politics fuel images of Japanese Americans and blacks as antagonistic competitors, we can also connect these images to more familiar ideas about the power of racial ideology in the struggles between labor and capital in the United States. I argue that the relationships between Japanese Americans and blacks have been important to the race/class hierarchies that have divided American labor, precisely because a coalition between Japanese Americans and blacks threatens the ideological and material mechanisms of American racism. My approach shows how Japanese Americans' positions in American race politics have been as much about the images in which Japanese Americans and blacks either appear together or in absentia as workers, consumers, and voters as they have been about the disenfranchising political and economic forces behind U.S. racism. At the same time I want to underscore the importance of multiple-pronged theoretical approaches in developing sophisticated understandings of how race works in the United States.

Moments

It was neither inevitable nor predictable that the connections between Japanese Americans and blacks would become so important to the way racial ideology and practice worked.[15] Neither is it surprising for Japanese American/black race politics theory to place civil rights and labor at its center, for these two areas have long been the locations where scholars of race have focused their attentions. The places where Japanese American and black histories converge are precisely where work, civil rights, and race intersect in American history.[16] At certain crossroads, the racial hierarchies that served the interests of those in political and economic power were threatened by isolated moments of interracial solidarity, periods when the ideology of racial hierarchies was affected by critical economic and political changes. Japanese American race politics theory must look for those points when the connections among Japanese Americans, blacks, labor, and politics were changing and affecting everyday life. Three instances where these connections can be seen clearly— moments when major political and economic shifts were taking place throughout the country—are (1) the arrival of Japanese and black workers to the West Coast around the turn of the century, (2) responses to Japanese American Internment during World War II, and (3) the Japanese American redress movement of the 1980s.

Japanese and blacks on the West Coast during the early twentieth century shared limited employment opportunities. Local restrictions kept Japanese in agriculture or small businesses and kept black populations in San Francisco or Los Angeles until after World War II. Like many others who arrived before and after them, Japanese American and black American workers in the new West experienced limited opportunities in domestic, agricultural, and railroad sectors.[17] Both groups arrived in California, Oregon, and Washington in numbers that were relatively small, yet a significant increase over those before 1910.[18] Despite the small numbers, the importance of both groups to the changing politics and economics of the West Coast was massive. Where before nonwhites had been mainly people of Native American, Mexican, or Chinese origin, the relatively small yet rapidly increasing population of Japanese and blacks changed the ways that white people on the West Coast thought about workers of color. The two groups came together after whites in labor organizations and abolitionist groups and white employers—whose fields, factories, railroads, and general stores were made productive by a variety of colored men and women—had argued loudly and vehemently over what was to be gained or lost when comparing Chinese exclusion to Negro slavery. Although the Chinese had "lost" and white wage workers had "won," it did not take long for the Chinese to be replaced. Black, Japanese, Mexican, and Italian migrants took the Chinese laborers' places as the competition that white workers despised and white employers exploited as cheap sources of labor. If the Mississippi Delta and its hard way of life was the birthplace of the blues, then the West Coast and the promises of opportunity it held for Japanese and black workers—with the price of racial discrimination—was the birthplace of Japanese/black race politics.

The iron horse as a symbol of the industrialization and westward expansion of the late nineteenth and early twentieth centuries was an extremely powerful and financially profitable technological force. Yet the effects on American society that steam engine technology helped to create—whether the development of racial hierarchies among railroad workers, the thousands of Chinese laborers who built the tracks and lost their lives while doing it, or the hundreds of "wrong side of the tracks" communities that developed in the railroad towns west of the Mississippi—tended to pit those who had the least against each other. This was the beginning of the history of Japanese Americans and blacks facing real-life labor realities, instigated in part by America's confidence in free markets and labor competition. The unfettered exploitation of the American labor force, courtesy of divisive racial hierarchies, gained a boost from Japanese American/black relations. Japanese Americans and blacks came together in America's new West Coast at a time when twentieth-century patterns of dealing with labor were being formed. Looking for opportunities to avoid the old patterns of feudalism and slavery, Japanese Americans and blacks may have left the old ways behind, but they quickly became integral parts of America's twentieth-century history of using politics and racial tension to turn workers' attention away from the dislocation and exploitation that the racial hierarchies maintained.

The lack of response to Japanese American Internment during World War II by America's leading Jewish and black civil rights organizations was one of the most defining, though rarely discussed, moments in Japanese American history. When President Roosevelt signed Executive Order 9066 on February 19, 1942, he OK'd the four-year evacuation, internment, and relocation of Japanese people living on the West Coast. Just as "the slavery experience" and "life on the reservation" have come to define African American and Native American communities, so has the forced internment during World War II come to define Japanese American experience. The forced removal of 120,000 Japanese Americans from the West Coast to desolate rural areas in the "interior" was in fact an unprecedented moment in U.S. civil rights history.[19]

Beyond the incredible violation of civil liberties—the majority of the 120,000 who were interned from 1942 to 1946 were American citizens who had done nothing wrong—Internment added to an environment that helped to foster the tensions among nonwhites and Jews that we see today. By not publicly recognizing the racism behind Internment and instead embracing the Roosevelt administration's propaganda that it was a matter of national security, black and Jewish civil rights organizations did not or could not rally behind Japanese Americans. These actions may not have solely altered the way that civil rights struggles played themselves out for most of the postwar era, but they do explain why Japanese Americans and blacks, in particular, are now portrayed in national imagery as polar examples of minority political action. The lack of response by minority civil rights organizations helped to ensure that Japanese Americans would be factored out of the civil rights movement—a turn of events that has repercussions today, as Japanese Americans and blacks now represent two of the most important places in U.S. civil rights history. These actions helped to ensure that the black/Jewish alliances, which gained strength during the war and became a powerful force later in the civil rights movement, would not become black/Jewish/Japanese alliances.[20]

Just as the Internment of Japanese Americans was a defining moment in Japanese American history, so was the redress and reparations movement. Beginning in 1970 and ending with the Civil Liberties Act of 1988,

Japanese Americans' campaign for redress seems to have replaced Internment as the research subject of choice for Japanese Americanist scholars.[21] When President Ronald Reagan signed H.R. 442 in August 1988, which in turn enacted the Civil Liberties Act of 1988, he appeared to be giving closure to a very painful part of Japanese American and U.S. history. The U.S. Congress and the American public agreed that Japanese Americans, and a small number of Aleutian Islanders, had been treated unjustly by the government and deserved to be compensated for their loss. A new federal office was created—the Office of Redress Administration—to hand out the $20,000-per-person reparations payment for what was estimated at the time to be around seventy-five thousand former internees. Although only tokens, the payments and written apology from the government to Japanese American communities were sweet contrasts to the unprecedented version of racism and violations of civil rights that Japanese Americans had suffered. Yet on the other hand, redress reflects something more than a bittersweet ending to an ugly moment. How redress was won, despite incredible political and economic obstacles, by casting Japanese Americans as "most favored minority"—and that it can be read as proof that race is an outdated concept and inapplicable to Asian Americans—complicates this Japanese American victory. The Japanese American redress movement may be seen as having brought closure to Internment and opening up new possibilities for the study of Asian American history, yet it must also be recognized for its place in the contemporary incarnations of Japanese American/black race politics that reinforce racial hierarchies more than ever before.

Redress was packaged to show that Japanese Americans were not like any other minority group. In other words, the redress movement would not set a precedent for future claims, because Internment was neither like commercial black enslavement nor like broken Native American treaties. Forced to justify redress by antagonistic opposition, Japanese American organizations and individuals fought back by lobbying from the position that Japanese Americans had been the only group to experience evacuation and internment. This is indeed true, but casting redress in such a light encouraged a distinction between Japanese Americans and others who had been discriminated against. Internment was different; it was about citizenship and not race.[22] This distinction may have been part of the reason why the NAACP was the only major civil rights organization that did not endorse the legislative campaign for redress, although the Black Congressional Caucus did give its support. With arguments for redress framed in such a way, at a time when black welfare queens and Native American indigenous sovereignty were considered major problems facing the federal government, the scene was set for Japanese Americans to become, unwittingly I believe, America's most favored minority.[23] With Japanese Americans in such a position, it was easy for Americans to believe that if there was just cause to correct discrimination, it should be done. Yet there was an important stipulation: only if the situation and those asking for it deserved it. The question of deserving and undeserving would plague political discourse long after the Japanese American victory, but its place within such debates is a critical one. The passage of H.R. 442, as a matter of citizenship and not racism, was indeed a turning point in U.S. race history because of its promise to set a precedent for cases from blacks and Native Americans. The act passed in part because it did not threaten racial hierarchies. We must take into consideration the possibility that the Civil Liberties Act of 1988 passed because it could be interpreted as fostering the kind of antagonism and jealousy among the poor, people of color, and women that fueled more recent campaigns to end affirmative action and welfare as we knew them.

Once H.R. 442 was signed, Japanese Americans took a strange place in U.S. race politics—a position that no other ethnic, religious, or racial group has yet to occupy. Through the redress movement, Japanese Americans set a precedent for others to wage similar movements. In fact, during the Congressional debates in 1988, this was a major concern for many lawmakers, who cringed at the possibilities of retribution claims from blacks and Native Americans, who could easily call for reparations. But even as the passage of the Civil Liberties Act of 1988 seemed to open up new possibilities for people of color, it also gave the American public a collective feeling of relief. With the Japanese American situation settled, even if some conservative members of Congress and their constituents did not approve, it was easy to believe that race no longer mattered in the United States. This was a formative moment in U.S. race politics, not just because of its importance to Japanese Americans, but also because it was a time of conflicting public opinions about how the nation would deal with minorities. I believe that it was no coincidence that H.R. 442 was signed by one of the most anti-civil-rights presidents of the postwar era. In a period when Reaganomics, free enterprise zones, and ketchup's promotion to vegetable status in federally funded school lunches were symbols in a nation where the rich were becoming richer faster than ever before, Japanese Americans were deemed the only group of "others" who merited attention from the federal government.

Just as in the cases of employment in the "New West" and civil rights organizations' reactions to Executive Order 9066, redress was connected to the political and economic changes in which it was embedded. In the case of redress, it came about at a time when the terms "identity politics" and "political correctness" were in their infancies and Jesse Jackson's Rainbow Coalition threatened to change the ways that disenfranchised Americans from a variety of backgrounds voted. Coalitions among discriminated groups were being developed in ways that they had never been before, as a result of the harsh economic and political policies of the Reagan era.

When we talk about landmark cases in U.S. civil rights, we should also remember that none of these cases stands alone. None of these decisions severed the connections among nonwhites; they strengthened them. When California segregated public school students according to race in 1860, "Asians, blacks, and Native Americans" were barred from schools for whites. And when the Supreme Court ruled in *Brown v. Board of Education* in 1954, it overturned laws passed in California and in Mississippi *(Gong Lum v. Rice)* in 1927 that legalized Asian American children's segregation. These cases were all extremely important in Asian American struggles for citizenship, but they also show how tightly woven and interdependent nonwhites' civil rights histories are in this country.

It was easy for Americans to think of the Civil Liberties Act of 1988 as Japanese American legislation, because they had already learned to think of the Civil Rights Act of 1964 as black legislation. When President George Bush signed his name to the letter that proclaimed that American traditions were being kept by the payment of reparations to a select group of Japanese Americans, he was correct. As much as the redress movement changed the Japanese American communities that sponsored it for the better and finally made public the injustice that the federal government had done to its own citizens, its passage helped to make sure that Japanese American/black racial politics stayed at the center of U.S. racial hierarchies.

Images

In the decades following World War II, magazines like *Life* and *National Geographic* shaped their readers' lives and the ways that they imagined their place in the world. And while during the postwar era generations of mainly white, middle-class readers learned about exotic people through photographs and the accompanying text, similar race magazines for Japanese Americans and blacks also presented a view of the world and of their readerships' changing places in it. Right after the end of the war, it was in these race magazines that the images of Japanese Americans and blacks turned up most frequently, reflecting their readers' concerns as well. The images that appeared in these publications, like those in *National Geographic,* provided a way to make comparisons between different groups, whether the audience was black, white, or Japanese American.[24]

So although images of Japanese Americans and blacks that were consumed by both white and nonwhite audiences may have been signs of their times, reflecting the cultural fads and quirks of the moment along with their readerships' changing lives, these publications are part of public memory. These images are the cultural artifacts that tell the story of Japanese, black, and white Americans gradually learning to rethink the differences between Japanese Americans and blacks, yet never forgetting that the two groups were at the center of ideas about race, class, and politics. For instance, the *Ebony* article that I mentioned earlier, "Of Jive and Japanese," detailed how blacks and Japanese Americans in Los Angeles' Japantown were getting along well, despite predictions that returning Japanese American internees and newly arrived blacks would not be able to share the same streets. But I want to concentrate on two stories, photo essays, that one lifestyle photo magazine, with a target audience of post-relocation Japanese Americans, used to create a frame of reference for its readership. Through the articles that appeared in *Scene* magazine during the early years following World War II, Japanese American audiences learned about their place in the world, courtesy of articles that highlighted Japanese American connections with blacks.[25]

From the late 1940s until the mid-1950s, *Scene* magazine, like other photo magazines of the day, presented stories that were both uplifting and to some extent political. The magazine, published, like *Ebony,* in Chicago, put out numerous articles showing Japanese American success in the years following Internment, along with national and international coverage of issues affecting Japanese Americans and Japan. Thus articles about the latest hairstyles for Japanese American young women in Chicago and the glamorous bachelor lifestyle of a Nisei bachelor architect in Crested Butte, Colorado, shared space with editorials about President Eisenhower's approach to Japan in light of the Korean War. However, one article about a Seattle multiracial football team and another about a Japanese American filmmaker stand out because of their treatment of Japanese American/black relations. They provide examples of the kinds of stories that helped create Japanese American/black race politics for Japanese American readers during the early postwar years.

In "Seattle's Little Big-Leaguers" (1953), *Scene* editors highlighted the story of a midget league football team in Seattle. The three-page article included more photos than text, yet stressed in both words and photos "a Nisei-Sansei-Filipino-Negro-white power combination." The series of photos that accompanied the story shows the boys, who were all thirteen or younger, off and on the field. A photo of an injured "Mickey Blakely, star Negro ball carrier of the 'Fighting Irish,'" being attended to by Japanese American coaches and surrounded by white and Asian American teammates shares space with another photo of the "team's secret weapon—12-year-old Takeshi Aoki." Perhaps one of the best photos shows the smiling boys holding up chopsticks at the Chinese dinner that their team sponsors paid for. The captions under the photos and the story's text make it clear that the piece was not only about the team's winning season, but about the positive benefits of a multiracial "power combination" off and on the gridiron.

This idea that Japanese American lives were tied in some ways to other nonwhites, blacks in particular, was made clear in an earlier story from 1949, "Africa Was Never Like That!" In this article, Toge Fujihara's experiences as a Nisei moviemaker in Liberia for Lutheran and Methodist churches in the United States were highlighted. What makes this article so interesting is the way that it makes both favorable and unfavorable comparisons between Japanese Americans and blacks—both Liberians and black Americans. Captions under the photos suggest a universality among different people. So readers learn of how "native housewives, like women the world over, swap gossip as they go shopping at the marketplace" and also how Toge "made a big hit with the natives when he took his turn at cooking rice, which they boil Japanese style." This rice cooking was explained as a way that the natives learned to deal with Toge, since "he wasn't a black man, but he wasn't quite like whites either." Articles like these portrayed a world to Japanese Americans in which being Japanese American was tied to other people of color (fellow citizens or Africans half a world away) in positive ways. I am not suggesting that these articles and others like them represent some golden age of Japanese/black identity. What I do believe is that such articles are examples of the ways that Japanese Americans in the early postwar years were seeing themselves depicted and what images Japanese American "lifestyle magazines" offered up to their readers.

The connections between Japanese Americans and other nonwhites (black Americans in particular) did not show up only in race magazines like *Scene* and *Ebony*. Mainstream readers could see the two groups in tandem in a variety of publications in the years on either side of World War II. Before World War II, fiction like *Pride of Palomar* (Kyne 1935) and *Seed of the Sun* (Irwin 1921), both of which were popular anti-Japanese pulp novels, argued that Jim Crow laws should be instituted for Japanese in the West or compared Japanese agricultural workers to Negro workers in the South. In 1950 Lait and Mortimer wrote *Chicago Confidential,* the Chicago edition in a series of best-selling "confidential raced tour guides." The book included chapters that highlighted the voracious sexual appetites of Japanese American women and black men for the fun-seeking Chicago tourist. The book's two white male authors advised their readers to be on the lookout for these sexual appetites anytime they visited Chicago.

Special issues in magazines and newspapers over the past thirty years have responded to public anxiety over minority demands for political, economic, and cultural equality.[26] These stories have created a public identification with Japanese American/black race politics among the public, even though few people outwardly speak of it. They have tended to stress that urban politics are troublesome, courtesy of the examples that Japanese Americans and blacks provide. Or in some cases they have portrayed Japanese American/black relations as Asian American/black relations and offered up images of antagonistic fighting over resources in urban areas, even as today the Asian/black conflict has been portrayed most often as a Korean/black issue.

One of the earliest examples of the "special issue effect" is found in *Cities in Trouble* (Glazer 1970). The book included reprints from a variety of sources, many of them from the *New York Times Magazine*. Of its numerous sections, it is the "Negro and the Immigrant" section that is notable. In a book devoted to addressing the ways that U.S. cities are in trouble, what group does the "Negro in the American city" get compared to? Japanese Americans. The section's introduction explains that Japanese Americans need to be compared to blacks, even though this "may seem strange in a collection devoted to urban problems." Two of the three articles in the section came from special reports that ran in January and September 1966. William Petersen's "Success Story, Japanese-American Style," which paints a picture of how Japanese Americans stand out in stark contrast to hippies, blacks, and Mexicans, and Irving Kristol's "The Negro Today Is Like the Immigrant Yesterday," which concludes on the basis of Japanese Americans' experiences that blacks should not use aggressive campaigns and activism to erase inequality but instead should follow Japanese Americans' practice of patience, are examples of the power of the special report to American audiences. These articles play off what at the time were national fears about the crisis of civil rights and demands for equality and justice being made by minorities, women, and "hippies." In a book about what was implied to be bad things going on in U.S. cities, an entire section was devoted to Japanese American and black experiences as indicators of urban politics—the kind that threatened stability and traditions of overcoming poverty and discrimination.

In Chicago more recently, special issues have also employed Japanese American/black American imagery to make larger statements about urban politics and race. From 1992 to 1993 the *Chicago Reporter* focused on Japanese American/black politics in its special series on Asian Americans in Chicago. Although the *Reporter* is a monthly newspaper, known as being a pro-poor-and-people-of-color publication, the articles that showed up periodically throughout the twelve months of the series tended to focus on the differences between Asian Americans and blacks. In two articles in the series, one on political redistricting and another on the changing racial makeup of Chicago's suburbs, Japanese American/black comparisons were either mentioned outright or implied.

The newspaper's attention to "troubled" Japanese American/black relations began with a story that appeared in the December 1992 edition. In an article entitled "Asian Americans Buck the Odds in Battle for Political Power," the paper pointed out that Asian and Latino Chicagoans did not have the benefit of reapportionment to increase their political power.

The article underscored that this was very different from blacks, who had benefited greatly from the redrawing of voting districts mandated by federal law. The article quoted both black and Asian American leaders (mainly Japanese American community leaders) as believing that having your "own kind" in positions of leadership was the best possible solution for achieving political equality.[27] What the readers of these various publications picked up from these links is uncertain. How their worlds were shaped by reading about and seeing photos of Japanese Americans and blacks is important, but not exactly the point here. What is critical is that these images directed readers' attention to Japanese American/black relations in a variety of contexts. It was not until the 1960s, when the nation's collective eye was directed toward civil rights, that the comparisons and contrasts began to make clear distinctions between the two groups.

Namaste

In the 1946 *Guide to Race Relations for Police Officers*, a California Department of Justice police training publication, officers were reminded that in order to be professional they should avoid "[u]se of expressions which may antagonize members of racial, religious, or other groups, such as 'nigger,' 'kike,' 'wop,' 'cholo,' 'chink,' 'chili-picker,' 'Jap,' etc." (State of California Department of Justice 1946: 13). Appearing just one year after World War II had ended and in the state that was one of the most outspoken in the calls for Japanese American internment, the guide is a study in words, images, public opinions, and seemingly rapid change over time. Japanese Americans' place in race politics can never be thought of in simple terms.

It seems as if I lived my entire academic career in the midst of one of the biggest intellectual duels of the twentieth century. Where exactly I fit within the nasty arguments and fights over intellectual authenticity probably depends on who is judging. I am drawn as much to the images of the Japanese American/black relationship as I am to the raced realities that created them. But at the same time, as much as the seductive newspaper headlines, magazine covers, and movie reviews call out to be analyzed and deconstructed, there can be no turning away from the material realities that buttress such images. There cannot be a dichotomy of analyses, no matter what the current fashion or faction of thought that demands a pledge of allegiance in exchange for admittance to a particular group of theorists. Identity cannot exist without a paycheck, and a bank account alone cannot explain why "yellow is neither white nor black." What I locate and define as Japanese American/black race politics serves a variety of causes and interests. In what follows, images of Japanese Americans and blacks simultaneously reflect and contradict (not to mention shape) Japanese Americans' shifting position in American race/class politics, even as Americans of every sort have come to accept that race is about black problems. Over the past century Americans have been taught to conceive of something that I call Japanese American/black race politics. A majority of the images of such politics in newspapers, books, and magazines over the past century have portrayed the two groups as competitors for the status of best workers and deserving participants in mainstream respectability, and in doing so helped to nearly eradicate any possibility for Japanese American/black coalitions. This is supported by an important minority of images and accounts that also appeared for popular consumption, particularly during and right after World War II. These images reflected the reality of the discrimination and manipulation by government policies and business hiring practices that Japanese American and black workers in the United States have continued to share, although today Japanese Americans have been "given" the economic advantage and blacks have been assigned the political advantage. Yet even these points of equilibrium are challenged by the redress movement of Japanese Americans and the growing black middle and upper middle class.

These public identities of Japanese Americans as masters of economic power and blacks as masters of political power squelch most possibilities for any cooperation between the two groups. The politics are as much about the image as they are about the reality, because there have been moments in U.S. history when the images and the realities converged and Japanese American/black race politics challenged existing racial hierarchies. Japanese Americans and blacks (and the psychological positions the two groups hold in national conceptions of race, work, and politics) are inherent components of how race and "whiteness" exist in the past, present, and future. Locating, defining, and telling the story of Japanese American/black race relations does not privilege one group at the expense of the other.

FIELD NOTES

July 6, 1996

When I entered the outer lobby of Heiwa Terrace, a group of elderly Asian American residents were coming in at the same time. As in many buildings with security systems, the outer lobby had a telephone and a video system for residents to let their guests into the building. The man and two women did not seem to pay much attention to me. I noticed a new sign on the security door: "Don't let anyone follow in behind you." It had never been there before during the year that I had been coming to Heiwa Terrace.

I called Bill's apartment to let him know that I had arrived. But before he could buzz me in, one of the two women in the group smiled at me and motioned for me to come through the door. I followed the group to the elevator, past the black man dozing at the security desk, pressed the button for Bill's floor, and got off a couple of floors before they did. I saw another Asian American resident walking down the hallway; he looked slightly frightened. An elderly white woman walked toward the elevator. When I turned to knock on Bill's door, I noticed that she was watching me.

When I got to Bill's room, he had his television on and was watching the video security camera channel. I had never seen the video feed before, either. I asked him what was going on, and he pointed to the screen and said, "I can see everything that goes on by looking at the screen." As we sat there and talked, a couple of times he would stop and point various residents out to me as they entered or left the building. He had started monitoring the station more often because of what happened a few nights before. He told me that on July 3 a black man followed one of the residents up to his room. The assailant had pulled out the man's telephone and "slugged him." Bill is

34

unsure whether or not the man will survive, because he was still in critical condition three days later.

Bill says that he has reached the point where he "doesn't want to be within arm's reach of any colored person, because of that kind of trouble." He did add with a laugh that he didn't mean me. I told him that I wasn't going to steal anything. We laughed. I told him about the people on his hallway that had seemed frightened by my appearance and said I hoped that security would not show up at the door and drag me away. He told me that he put up the sign in the lobby telling people to look behind them. He complained that he had been watching and had noticed that people just don't look behind them and that they had to be more careful about who followed in behind them. I didn't have the heart to tell him how easily I had been let in the building.

CHAPTER TWO

An Embarrassment of Riches

> I think that in the future such projects of research that... have the
> present quality of muddling through, having started off with very
> different assumptions and expectations, will be very much a matter
> of design and innovation as anthropology revises its emblematic
> methods. Is this anthropology any less scientific than it has ever
> been? I think not. In any case, it need not be.
> —George Marcus, *Ethnography through Thick and Thin*

> I suggest here that one's positioning within marginalized
> communities—of ethnic, race, religion, or gender—shapes not only
> one's research interest and the epistemologies one chooses in
> developing such research, it also sensitizes one in conscious and/or
> unconscious ways to look at practices of exclusion and perhaps to
> write in ways that do not accept the status quo. I say "perhaps"
> because it is clearly a more entangled subject.
> —Pnina Motzafi-Haller, "Writing Birthright"

There is a box pushed under my desk that contains about two dozen audiotapes and a large spiral-bound notebook: these are the interviews and field notes from a year and a half of fieldwork in Chicago. These data were never supposed to go unused. On the contrary, I had planned that this information would be at the center of what would become my doctoral dissertation. At the beginning of my research I had every intention of conducting a study of the Japanese national community in Chicago. My research design centered around the question of what it meant to be "Japanese" in Chicago in the 1990s and how Japanese nationals experienced race while living in the United States.[1] I used my connections as a former Japanese government employee to obligate consulate employees to agree to my interviews. I did the same at a suburban elementary school run by the Japanese government for Japanese nationals. Some of my interviews grew out of my friendship with the principal of the school and his ability to "obligate" my interviews with teachers. Operating within these government circles, I attended parties, networking events, and conferences held for and by Japanese nationals in the Chicago metropolitan area. I was able to befriend a Japanese woman who worked illegally as a waitress at these events. Through her I got to know her husband and some of his coworkers. These men were part of one of the rarely recognized or discussed groups of Japanese nationals living in major U.S. cities—Japanese citizens who work on contract in expensive Japanese restaurants for relatively low wages.[2] In addition, through an American woman I had known in Japan, I became friendly with a group of Japanese housewives who lived on Chicago's North Shore. And over Christmas break in 1993, I worked at Chicago's famous Marshall Field's department store and shocked many of the mostly female Japanese customers with my Japanese language and etiquette. I took advantage of their surprise and asked many of them if I could interview them for my research. Five of these women agreed. I felt lucky to have such willing groups of Japanese citizens who, even if acting out of obligation or boredom, were helping to make my fieldwork a success.

Sometime during this period my ideas about the production of anthropological knowledge began to change. I started to seriously rethink the questions I was asking and where I was looking for their answers. I realized that I could not argue confidently about Japanese nationals in the United States in the present if I did not have some knowledge of Japanese Americans in the past. To satisfy this requirement I began searching out the earliest accounts of Japanese nationals in Chicago. I searched in public libraries in the metropolitan area and the Chicago Historical Society's collections. As I learned more about Japan's role in the racial politics surrounding Chicago's 1893 Columbian Exposition, I became more curious about Chicago's role in Japanese American history during and right after World War II. After about a month and a half of this research I was past the point of wondering if the growing incredible wealth of data that I was gathering concerning Japanese Americans in Chicago was true. I desperately wanted to find out from living people if what I was reading about the entwined stories of Japanese Americans and the black/white color line in Chicago was accurate. I knew that the Japanese American Citizen's League (JACL) office was just four blocks away from my apartment, but had no idea whom I should contact. One day I asked a graduate student colleague who was active in the JACL if she had any ideas on how to locate Nisei who might agree to be interviewed. She gave me a name, and after a series of telephone calls and meetings with

board members, the second phase of my fieldwork was under way. Toward the beginning of 1995, I began interviewing the Nisei members of
the Japanese American Citizen's League Human Rights Committee.

Despite the fact that the earliest phase of my fieldwork is not at the
center of this research, it is neither forgotten nor ignored. Although its
influence is not explicit here, the first leg of fieldwork has a significant
role. My decision to put it aside came from the urgency I began to feel
from the first meetings that I had with the JACL members. In 1995, when
I decided to locate Japanese Americans who could tell me what it had
been like to cross Chicago's color line and if they felt that they really
had, I began to build another rich stash of tapes and field notes and a set
of generous friends whom I admittedly must also call informants. I was
indeed lucky to have such a wealth of research to choose from, even if at
least a quarter of it does not appear in the body of this text. Realizing that
ethnography is both fieldwork and interpretation, this shift was not just
a change from one group of informants to another. It was a major development in my understanding of my place in debates over the production of anthropological knowledge, race studies, and Asian American
scholarship. Expanding my fieldwork from concentrating on Japanese
nationals to a diffusion of archival materials and elderly Nisei influenced
not only how I conducted my research but also how I came to interpret it.

I do not believe that I am alone among anthropologists in the shifting
of my focus during the course of my fieldwork. Even after we determine
that our fieldwork is finished, we still must make something of our data.
These choices are what make the production of ethnography a skill—
complete with proven techniques and procedures.

The question of constructing an anthropological self, placing oneself
in the text, blurring genres, or any of the other nontraditional anthropological methods of writing an ethnography is a luxury to which I pay
close attention. Perhaps surprisingly, I have little tolerance for those who
seem not only to place themselves in the text but also to make themselves
the center. But throughout my fieldwork and the process of working
through the data that it produced, I could not escape the issue of why it
was that the questions I was asking about Japanese American/black connections in the past and present were not more common, given the incredible materials and life histories that I was finding. Of course I secretly
knew why I had happened upon this rich vein of information. It was in
part because of my own position in the field of anthropology and in

everyday life that I had asked the type of questions that produced the possibility to rethink so many assumptions about Japanese Americans and blacks, the black/white race model, and the ways that elderly non-white Americans think about race. It would be foolish to deny that my experiences—growing up in a predominately white suburb and knowing that Chicago was where the "action" was, living in Japan for more than two years, building friendships with history graduate students who taught me their methodologies, and a close relationship with my maternal grandmother—have no relevance to what appears here. Similarly, it would be difficult not to admit that this work is firmly grounded in more traditional approaches toward anthropological research.

The eye through which I have conducted this research could never be thought of as neutral. The autoethnographical methods that I use here—raw field-note entries, making connections between my own life and the lives of my subjects, ruminations about my position as a "double-crosser," or my concerns and frustration about what I see as self-serving academic proponents of the black/white race model in the United States—seem to me necessary admissions in understanding how this work has been put together. I also know that the importance of my personal experiences, both before and during my fieldwork, to the type of questions I asked and what I observed is not a license to make this ethnography "mine." By this I mean that I cannot, and have tried not to, make my ethnographic voice the center of attention. I do not believe that by virtue of my minority status I am more attuned to the complexities of Japanese American/black race theory than a white man in his fifties would be. As I weave my informants' personal narratives and oral histories with historical documents and my ethnographic fieldwork, I have tried to think about my research and its place within and outside of academic contexts and to present an honest and rigorous analysis of my experiences in the field and the data that came out of them.

In the Field

From 1992 until 1996 I lived in the Andersonville section of the Edgewater neighborhood on Chicago's Far North Side.[3] Unlike many anthropologists who go "to the field," I had already been living there for three years when I began my formal interviews and archival research. Because my family lived in a western suburb, I had lived in or near the Chicago metropolitan area for twenty-five years. The switch from resident to researcher has its benefits and its costs. The stage for conducting my research had been in the making for years. I knew so much, too much, and too little—all at the same time. What follows is a description of my field site, my fieldwork, and my key informants, as influenced by my change from resident to resident ethnographer.

When I conducted my fieldwork in the late 1990s, Chicago's population was around 3 million, with an additional 4 million people living in its suburbs. The city's racial breakdown was 45.4 percent white, 39.1 percent black, 3.7 percent Asian, and .3 percent Native American.[4] During the time that I lived on the North Side it seemed as if many of these people had decided to relocate to the Edgewater neighborhood—as well as Uptown to the south, Rogers Park to the north, and the Ravenswood district of Lincoln Square to the west. Simplifying the complex processes of gentrification, these Far North Side neighborhoods were becoming too expensive for most of their current residents as more and more urban professionals (mostly white and under forty years old) saw these neighborhoods as desirable places to live. But the question of the relationship between desire and ability is a good one to ask here.

Between 1992 and 1996 apartment rents and home values on the Far North Side experienced some of the greatest increases in the city. I experienced this personally. When I first moved into my apartment, my rent was $425 per month. When I moved out in 1996, the same apartment was listed at $725 per month. Average home values showed even greater increases. In 1992 the average home value in Edgewater was $163,836, but by 1996 it was $215,829. The small Lakewood-Balmoral section of Edgewater that was just a block away from my apartment building experienced tremendous increases. During this same period, average home values went from $164,339 to $315,478. Similar increases took place in Uptown and Ravenswood, although they were not as great as those in Lakewood-Balmoral. Rogers Park to the north, on the boundary with the upscale suburb of Evanston, was the only Far North Side neighborhood that was below citywide averages—increasing from $170,363 to $177,484. The Chicago average went from $190,404 to $208,043 over the same four-year period. In a neighborhood where 73 percent of the households were renters, these increases were changing the dynamics of desire and ability to live on the Far North Side.[5]

Even without firsthand knowledge of such statistics, the changes taking place in these neighborhoods are obvious. From Uptown's southern

Figure 4. Boarded-up building waiting for rehabbing in the Edgewater neighborhood.

border to Rogers Park's northern border with Evanston, blond and red-bricked buildings built in the teens and twenties are being gutted and rehabbed. Some of these buildings were slums, but others were simply well-kept, decent housing. The question of where the buildings' former residents go when the signs go up announcing the opportunity to buy a condominium, in buildings with grand names like "The Chelsea" or "The Atriums of Andersonville," is unclear. But the signs on the buildings indicate that their former residents would not be able to afford them. It would have been difficult in 1996 to find a condo that was priced at less than $180,000. The grand three- and four-flat buildings or the larger apartments in these neighborhoods that were created by conversions of turn-of-the-century, single-family Victorians during Chicago's housing shortage in the 1940s and 1950s are now in demand among those who themselves cannot afford to live closer to downtown. The hardwood floors, ornate ceramic tiles, and trademark Chicago back porches (part of the building code since the famous 1871 fire) of these buildings are beautiful. And the tree-lined streets of the Far North Side that are tucked off the major streets easily resemble a town from a Sinclair Lewis novel or 1950s sitcom. Community groups in some of the more expensive blocks are well organized. They plant flowers on corners and run organized block watches. Less than thirty minutes away from the Loop (Chicago's downtown) by mass transit and with easy access to Lake Shore Drive, it is understandable why these are desired neighborhoods.

The hidden story behind almost every gentrification in process, especially that taking place on the Far North Side, is that the area has gone through a series of changes in racial and economic demographics. At the beginning of the twentieth century these were Chicago's suburbs—recently developed farmlands. By the middle of the century these areas had been incorporated into Chicago proper and were a mix of Chicago's cosmopolitan flavor and good living. During the early years of U.S. cinema, many movie studios operated in Uptown, including ones run by Charlie Chaplin and pioneer black filmmaker Oscar Michaeux. Streetcars from downtown brought residents, shoppers, and thrill seekers to the area's clubs and shopping districts. These were the good old days for the Far North Side.

Margate Park is one of the few places in these neighborhoods that has remained white and wealthy throughout the twentieth century. The district is officially part of Uptown, but has always been a wealthy white enclave since its stately homes were built in the 1890s. Yet even when Uptown was 99 percent white in 1940, Margate Park had a high concentration of the .2 percent of blacks listed as Uptown residents in the 1940 census. The small but longtime group of black residents who made up Margate Park's domestic workforce were allowed to live on one block of modest homes in close proximity to their employers. But after World War II, Uptown, Edgewater, and Rogers Park gradually began to change with regard to race and class. Japanese American relocatees led the way for Native Americans and blacks, who arrived in lesser numbers. By 1950, the neighborhoods were home to large pockets of Appalachian whites and Native Americans, who were encouraged by social welfare agencies and cheap rents to the Far North Side apartments that had been created from homes and larger apartments in the scramble to increase the number of housing units.[6] By the 1970s many, but not all, of the wealthy and middle-class white residents had moved to the suburbs or died. It was then that many community groups formed in protest against the area's high concentration of halfway houses and transient hotels. The area had become attractive to the federal government, and a large number of HUD-backed Section 8 housing developments were built. Some were high-rise, but others were built to look like town homes. Many of the high-rises were built exclusively for the elderly.

The area also became one of Chicago's most ethnically diverse and international areas during this time. Today, as the area has begun to appeal to the grandchildren of earlier white residents who fled its changing demographics, it has become the site of large concentrations of immigrants from Southeast Asia, Latin America, the Caribbean, West Africa, and Eastern Europe who can afford the slowly increasing rents. In 1990 in Edgewater, 18,000 foreign residents lived next door to, shopped with, and attended school with 43,000 native-born residents. Contrary to the stereotypical image of Chicago as a city of stark racial contrasts, the Far North Side neighborhoods in the 1990s were made up of pockets of varied wealth, race, sexuality, and nationality.

While I conducted my fieldwork I lived in one of these pockets. My building of three one-bedroom apartments on one side and six two-bedroom units on the other was one of the few apartment buildings in Andersonville. For the most part, most of my neighbors in the building were under thirty-five and either single or single with roommates. I was the only black person in my building; however, one of my neighbors had a Filipina mother and a white father. She worked in downtown Chicago as an administrative assistant and was in her mid-twenties. The white couple who lived above me were in their late thirties. She worked at a department store selling cosmetics and he was a sales representative who aspired to be a professional opera singer. When compared with the rest of Andersonville, my building's demographics seemed representative.

On summer evenings when many residents would hang out on their stoops talking to neighbors or on winter days when everyone seemed to be out shoveling sidewalks and commenting on how cold the weather was, Andersonville often looked like an advertisement for the new urban America. The neighborhood was full of young, hip residents who appreciated the art galleries, ethnic restaurants, coffeehouses, progressive bookstores, and "small town in the big city" atmosphere. But the reality is that, outside the Andersonville section, Edgewater is not like Andersonville. In 1990, 14 percent of Edgewater's households were classified as "aged living alone." And while 58 percent of Edgewater's residents were white, 19 percent were black, 17 percent were Hispanic, and 12 percent were listed as "other."[7] Andersonville is surrounded by this other Edgewater. When Andersonville's residents get off the train or bus and walk home they are in this other Edgewater. Trips to the grocery store, cleaners, video store, or café make this other Edgewater's existence undeniable.

When a new produce chain opened up a store on Broadway just east of Andersonville, I stopped in for its grand opening celebration every day for almost two weeks. The shoppers represented the many different people who live in Andersonville. The market's selection of quality merchandise, from oranges to Filipino sausages to upscale imported Italian canned tomatoes, was priced much cheaper than anything else around for miles. The new store made it clear that just as economics kept the pockets apart, economics brought them together.

Along the lakefront, on the eastern side of Broadway, is one part of the other Edgewater outside of Andersonville. It is where Eastern European men and women in their seventies and eighties share the lakefront paths with Haitian children on bikes and Ecuadorian soccer players. It is also where the police who serve this part of the North Side are dispatched most often. I learned this from borrowing my grandmother's police scanner one summer and listening with a mixture of shock, horror, and guilty voyeurism. On its western boundary Edgewater's population is a mixture of working-class Asian and Latino households. The area from Ashland Avenue westward to the Ravenswood rail line is a mixed residential/commercial pocket. Along the Ravenswood commuter rail line, small light industrial businesses and metalworking shops exist in a thin strip of former industrial buildings. Here, too, however, many of these businesses are leaving and the structures are being converted to high-priced residential loft spaces. In a neighborhood like Edgewater, in a pocket like Andersonville, buses and grocery store checkout lines are the only points of intersection for the diverse residents of what urban planners like to call a neighborhood in transition.

When I first approached the men and women whose lives are woven into this history of Japanese Americans in Chicago, I was worried. Even though I was an "other" asking to study other "others," I was familiar with what it might "look like" for me to go to "the Japanese American community." I didn't want to appear to be saying, "I am going to tell *your* people's story in *my* words and use my own lens of blackness to do it." Yet at the end of that first Chicago JACL Human Rights Committee meeting in the fall of 1995, each one of the men and women who were there agreed to my request.

I had found out about the Japanese American Citizen's League Human Rights Committee (HRC) through a graduate student colleague who belonged to the organization's board of directors. After going through a

Figure 5. Gentrification in progress in Uptown.

series of meetings explaining my project to board members and the board itself, I was allowed to meet with the Human Rights Committee, comprising mainly retired Nisei. The committee is part of the JACL and every year submits a budget to the JACL board of directors, yet from the beginning it was clear that the committee was one of the most controversial groups within the organization.

The HRC is a special committee within the Chicago chapter of the national Japanese American Citizen's League. The JACL was founded in 1929 and today is one of the largest and oldest Asian American organizations in the country. It has about 24,500 members in 112 chapters in twenty-five states. And although its headquarters is in San Francisco, there are regional offices in Los Angeles, Fresno, Chicago, and Seattle. The Chicago chapter is one of the largest local chapters, with 3,000 members. The HRC, with only 11 members, is a select group. Yet although their everyday activism represents a minority opinion about how to define Japanese American identity, the HRC members' individual and collective protests against discrimination cannot be downplayed. What makes the HRC special is its members. But what also makes it stand out is that it is the only active human rights organization among the 112 JACL chapters.[8] Whether it is that those who decided to stay in Chicago after the war tended to be more outspoken than others or that they live half a continent away from the heaviest concentrations of Japanese Americans, Chicago's Japanese American community is considered one

Figure 6. New construction side by side with "classic" Chicago apartment buildings, near Sheridan Road, Uptown.

of the most outspoken. Even the most famous moment in Japanese American activism, the redress movement, is in line with the Chicago tradition of dissension. The National Council for Japanese American Redress (NCJAR), centered in Chicago, was one of three groups working for redress and was the most confrontational.[9]

I wanted to be honest with the committee members about the personal reasons behind my request to interview them. I explained to them that I was doing this project because of my own embarrassment at never really knowing much about Japanese Americans, but also because I wanted to find evidence that would fill out what I was finding in my historical research. I told them that I hoped they could help me understand what it had been like during that transitional period after World War II when blacks and Japanese Americans were arriving in Chicago in record numbers. I proposed that I interview them and tape these conversations and, if possible, attend a few meetings to see how they made decisions about what causes to focus on. I told them that I would be sure to give them aliases and to do my best to protect their real identities.[10]

I also told them that I was doing this research with my own seventy-eight-year-old grandmother in mind. She had been injected with a distrust of Japanese during World War II. Her reactions to my going to work in Japan years before and, later, to my research on Japanese Americans had been the same. The Japs! I did not tell the committee that night, but it amazed me, then and now, that a loving woman who had been forced to deal with race prejudice because of her own "dubious" hue could still have such strong negative opinions about another group of "coloreds." This was especially strange to me because, although my grandmother knew about Japanese American Internment, she made it secondary to what she determined was "their" disdain for "us." That first night, I explained to the committee members that I wanted them to help me disprove what I continued to hear from my "people." Whenever I would mention my research to black friends, relatives, and strangers, I would get a response like, "They think that they are better than us."

As I explained all of this to the nine members of the committee who were in attendance that evening, I looked around at the men and women in the room. Officially the committee at that time had twelve members, although this number fluctuated from twelve to nine to fourteen during my research. There were no dropouts, but often trips to visit family or to activist events would take various members away from the group. Luckily for me, in attendance that first night were Dan Hayashi, the leader of the group, and Lois Chiaki. Dan is a retired minister who had been active in many civil rights struggles in the United States and Asia, and Lois is a Sansei from Hawaii who had been integral to my getting the opportunity to present my research goals to the committee. After I gave my presentation, Dan moved that the committee agree to be interviewed and to make me a member of the Human Rights Committee. Lois seconded it, and with little debate I was allowed in.

I began my interviews with the members and eventually found out that four of the committee members were the most eager and most willing to discuss their opinions of race in America openly. These members were ironically not Dan and Lois, however. During the course of my year and a half with the Human Rights Committee my key informants were Bill Murasaki, retired skilled laborer; Tom Watanabe, retired pharmacist; Al Kawaii, retired high school principal; and Rose Yamamura, retired personal assistant. They ranged in age from Bill at eighty to Rose at seventy. Only Al Kawaii lived with a spouse. The others lived alone, and like many of the Nisei generation, neither Rose nor Bill had married. All except for Bill lived in homes that they had owned for many years. The homes were modest yet well-kept Far North Side dwellings.

Bill Murasaki was born in San Francisco in 1915. He relocated to Chicago in 1945. Bill held many jobs in Chicago, including working for a short while as a dental X-ray technician at Stanley Park Hospital—a skill he learned in camp by reading the General Electric manual. He now lives in Heiwa Terrace, a HUD-subsidized apartment for the elderly in Uptown. The tall brown building, one of the numerous high-rise apartment buildings along Lake Shore Drive, has a small Japanese garden on its western corner and an even smaller parking lot on its eastern side. On the first floor there are three activity rooms and a dining room. The staff's main office is right off the central entrance. There are eight floors of apartments, each with its own kitchenette, bathroom, and bedroom. Bill's apartment is full of the many newspapers, magazines, and books that keep him one of the best informed of my interviewees. He has a large color television and two easy chairs, as well as a couch. Even though it's crammed, Bill's apartment is neat and spotless. Outside of Bill's apartment the hallways on the residential floors are covered in the kind of brown low-pile carpeting that can be found in many other public buildings. The carpet is much like Heiwa Terrace in general—clean and functional. On the first floor, residents' artwork is pasted on the walls throughout the halls. At least three hundred elderly residents live in the building, but the numbers constantly fluctuate and there is a waiting list to get an apartment there. Most of Bill's neighbors in Heiwa Terrace are either Japanese American or of other Asian ancestry. Yet there is a sprinkling of non-Asian residents, blacks and foreign-born whites, as well.

Tom Watanabe was one of the first Japanese Americans to arrive in Chicago in 1943. Tom had been a senior at the University of Southern California when World War II broke out. Tom and other Japanese American seniors at USC were allowed to graduate under special provisions set up by USC, getting credit for their final semester since they had been forced to leave school because of Executive Order 9066. So Tom received his degree in pharmaceutical science while he and his family were in an Internment camp in Poston, Arizona. After a year in the camp, Tom went to Chicago. He eventually married a Nisei woman, had three children, and became active in a wide variety of civil rights organizations. He is known among the committee for his involvement in the desegregation of Woolworth lunch counters in the South in the 1960s.

Tom has been a widower for many years, but has a close white woman friend from his activist days. He continues to live in the house he and his wife bought during the early years of resettlement. It is a grand blue house from the turn of the century, in good condition, with a large front porch and a beautiful front-yard garden. Inside Tom's home is the combination of well-worn furniture styles, lighting fixtures, and appliances that you might expect from someone who has lived in a house for almost fifty years. It is filled with handmade ceramics from his late wife and a few Japanese prints and sculptures. But Tom does not live in the past. During my visits he was quite handy with the microwave and would often produce pastries or hot beverages courtesy of his microwave oven.

Al Kawaii was born in 1924 and grew up in a rural town outside of Los Angeles. After serving in World War II, Al relocated to Chicago and eventually went to college and became a public school teacher in 1953. Al went on to become Chicago's first Asian American principal. His experiences in the school system have given Al an intense and keen perspective on race politics in Chicago. Al lives in the Rogers Park neighborhood with his wife. They have three children, none of whom has married a Japanese American. In his retirement Al is an avid golfer, but spends a great deal of time at local public schools giving presentations about Japanese American history, as well as participating in antidiscrimination programs.

Al's home is located on a major street in Rogers Park. Architecturally, it is a good example of the Chicago Craftsman style. It is surrounded by mature trees and flowers with a small yard in back. Inside, dark wood floors and paneling give it a warm, comfortable feeling. Al and I (sometimes joined by his wife, Ella) would often have lunch before our interviews. We would eat a combination of foods that Ella had prepared for us. These lunches reminded me a lot of Japan—a mixture of sandwiches, cold cuts, vegetables, noodles. Although I never saw more than the dining room, living room, and kitchen, I was surprised that despite Al's prominence in Chicago, I never saw any plaques, medallions, or trophies.

Rose Yamamura was born in 1925, the only daughter of a prosperous Portland, Oregon, businessman. Like Al, Rose is very much involved in the public school systems. She has appeared on local radio stations. Rose also teaches flower arranging in her home to a variety of students. Rose does all of this with few people knowing that she graduated with a degree in engineering from the University of Wisconsin in 1946. She was the only woman in many of her classes. Rose joined her parents in Chicago after her graduation, but was never able to find a job in her chosen field. After a series of jobs, including a long stint as a secretary with an exclusive private club, Rose finally "lucked out," she says, and became a personal assistant to a wealthy physician. Rose is one of the most outspoken of my informants, with strong convictions about civil rights and what she sees as Japanese American apathy about anything political.

Rose's home in Lakeview, like the homes of all my informants except Al, is an old home in good condition, but probably in need of an updated kitchen and a fresh coat of paint if it were to go on the real estate market. Yet, as a good example of the Chicago two-flat style in a highly desirable location, Rose's narrow, two-story brick building would certainly get top dollar if it were for sale. Rose lives on the top floor while renting out the bottom floor to a black male librarian. Because Rose teaches flower arrangement to a wide variety of students, her living room and dining room are set up to accommodate small groups of students. Rose lives alone, although she co-owned the house and lived there with her parents until they died. Rose's aesthetic style is showcased in her wonderful furniture, rugs, china, and vases. All of it is simple and tasteful and looks expensive. Rose does not have a lot, but what she has reflects her life on the fringes of the wealthy in Chicago.

Through these individuals, I was able to expand my interviews and meet their siblings and friends, whom they felt I "just had to talk to." We made appointments usually a month in advance and met almost every month. Our interviews were almost always at their homes—all of them except Bill have lived in the same homes for more than thirty years—and because all of them lived on the Far North Side, we often saw each other while running errands. During the warmer months when I rode my bicycle, I would often hear my name or see a wave and it would be one of the committee members. From the fall of 1995 to the winter of 1996 I conducted numerous interviews, but still kept coming back again and again to these four.

For the first two interviews, I would ask my interviewee to describe his or her life. I would tell my informants that life histories and kinship charts were important to anthropologists, but that they could tell me whatever they wanted in whatever form they wished. Although I tried not to go beyond my ninety-minute audiotapes, I would sometimes have to get another. Other times, I would turn off the tape recorder and we would just talk. In those cases, I would sometimes jot down later what we had spoken about, but usually would not. Sometimes I had to make a decision about whether or not I should consider a conversation about herbal remedies for arthritis to be important data.

Subsequent interviews would range from talking together about my latest archival find to discussing local, national, or international events. I would often ask someone to talk more about something mentioned in an earlier interview or to tell me how their picketing had gone the week before. I found that my informants were always eager to share their thoughts about a variety of topics. The only direction I would usually have to give to our one- to two-hour interviews would be at the beginning to get things started and at the end to make suggestions that we continue a given topic at our next session. I had at least five formal taped interviews with each of my key informants. In total I interviewed sixteen people for at least an hour or more, although as stated above my key informants contributed a larger percentage of my taped interviews than did the others.

In addition I attended the committee's monthly meetings and social events like the annual summer picnic at Lois's house, the yearly Intergenerational Dialogue, and the Scholarship Luncheon. Lois and her husband lived in Rogers Park in a tucked-away, difficult-to-reach street. We all sat around in lawn chairs in the side yard, and once again I was introduced to family and friends by the members with pride as "wanting to find out about Nisei activism." I went to two of the Human Rights Committee protests, although I did not take an active role in speaking at these events, as some of the members did. The transformation from researcher to participant observer to voting member took place sometime in January 1996. I found that I had mysteriously moved from being a researcher to a full-fledged committee member in the committee's eyes. I was not told or asked; it just happened. In this new status, which in some ways made me uneasy, knowing that I was both conducting research and taking part in an activist movement, I helped to draft committee statements and devise strategy. My opinions were always respected even though I was hesitant to offer them. That seemed to be taking the participant-observer role too far.

Throughout these meetings and the street protests, I openly took notes. Everyone saw me and knew that I was doing so. In a moment of horror, I received a call one day after a meeting. I had left my red notebook at the JACL headquarters. When I ran up to the office to get it, a JACL member I'd never met said he'd been wondering whose notes they were and figured they were mine. I never forgot my notebook again.

In the meetings and events that involved the larger Japanese American community, I used a tape recorder but asked the permission of the sponsoring organizations. I attended some of the various social events that were organized and put on by other Japanese American groups in the area. These included the yearly fundraiser at the Japanese American Service Committee in Uptown and special events offered at Heiwa Terrace, the retirement home in Uptown that, as its name implies, has a large Japanese American population.

The archival research of my project revolved around three separate archival collections. I had already spent a great deal of time in the special collections department of Chicago's Harold Washington Library when I was searching for information relevant to Japanese nationals at the Columbian Exposition in 1893. However, the downtown library's government collection and the Buena Park branch's neighborhood files were indispensable. Without question my research would not have taken the course that it did, nor would I have been encouraged to seek out the members of the Human Rights Committee, if not for the Chicago Historical Society's research library. Its collections of ephemera and dissertations related to Japanese Americans in Chicago and of Chicago Resettlers' Committee papers provided much of the historical material that lies at the backbone of this book. In addition, the private holdings of the Chicago Japanese American Historical Society and interviews with its curator provided me with rare copies of *Scene* magazine.

I defined my object of study through a traditional ethnographic eye that included gathering life histories through conventional methods. I used the "snowball method" of locating people to interview—asking every person I interviewed if he or she knew anyone else I should talk to. Because I had read so many traditional monographs, I was not surprised when these second interviewees were often the brothers, sisters, or coworkers of my informants. Their histories are interwoven throughout the work and make appearances not in the context of a traditional time line, but more in the context of their support of the book's fundamental premise—that Japanese American awareness of U.S. racial hierarchies is key to understanding the multiple effects of the color line on all of us.

The HRC members went beyond allowing me interviews; they invited me to all meetings and events held at various locations throughout the year. Not only was I the only black member, but I was also the youngest. I began to understand that their lives are unusual because of their activism and their "leftist" concerns. This is not just because they are Japanese Americans or senior citizens. It is that they have to varying degrees been political all their lives. Yet at the same time, as nonwhite residents of Chicago for the past fifty years, they are much like others of their generation who have lived most of their lives in U.S. urban areas. They have watched as good jobs with benefits left the city. They have seen the demographics of neighborhoods change around them. The people who allowed me to use their stories knew that it was not just being Japanese during a war with Japan that had allowed the Internment of Japanese Americans to take place. They were spending the end of their lives making sure that they didn't forget that it was a continuation of America's history of racial discrimination. They knew that their stories were also mine.

They have all told their stories and been interviewed before—some of them almost constantly. During my fieldwork two of them appeared in separate *Chicago Tribune* newspaper features, and I came across numerous references to their lives or photos in academic and popular articles. Yet they still allowed me into their organization and into their homes. Even as I asked them questions about their early lives before coming to Chicago, questions that I could tell by their body language and tone of voice they had been asked and had answered a million times before, they told me their stories. I suppose I did get some consolation from the fact that none of these previous researchers or interviewers had ever asked the "black" questions. No one was interested in finding out about Japanese American/black relations.

Of the fifteen Nisei whom I interviewed extensively, all seemed to sigh a kind of "OK, here we go again" when I would ask them to talk about their lives before they moved to Chicago. Some even handed me autobiographical life histories or articles from newspapers and books that included some other researcher's interviews and answers to questions about life before and during Internment. In each case, I would apologize and ask them to tell me again. But I would also ask at the beginning of each individual interview if anyone, in all the times that they had been interviewed, had ever asked them about Japanese Americans' lives in Chicago with respect to blacks and race. No one ever answered yes.[11]

On the Page

How do I describe what it feels like to be a turncoat? In the age of identity politics I run the risk of making a wide variety of groups and individuals angry by what I offer here. Even while I proudly don the hats of feminist anthropologist, black anthropologist, scholar of Asian American studies, "Japanologist," historian, and connoisseur of textual analysis, this book does not fit easily into any of these categories. A black woman with no traceable ancestry to Japan details how "model minorities" have unmodel pasts and presents. A black woman focuses on Japanese Americans in Chicago to argue that Americans should finally begin to speak and write about the black/white race model's power to divide and mask those who live within it. An anthropologist who relies on grainy microfilm of old race magazines as much as she does crackling audiotapes and worn notebooks filled with field notes must still show that she knows how to do ethnography.

I cannot turn away from what my research has shown to be a history of Japanese Americans in Chicago simultaneously supporting and challenging the way race and culture have been defined in the United States since World War II, nor can I ignore the ways I have tried to make sense of this history and my place within it as anthropologist. It is because I have attempted to do the type of research that I admire and believe in that I highlight shifts in Chicago neighborhoods' political and economic histories. Yet it is because my own life has been so noticeably shaped by the power of economic realities to rework racial definitions that I also spend entire sections attempting to figure out how "what it means to be Japanese" is tied to the symbolic idea of Chicago. As is very evident, I have been vastly influenced by social history and have thus tried to return the favor and write an ethnography that will appeal to historians who are attracted to ethnographic methodologies. And since there is no one chapter on "women" or on "culture" in a work about family and race politics, it is clear that I believe in muddying more than tidying.

When I decided to change my focus and stop interviewing Japanese nationals and follow what can only be described as informed feeling, I was worried. I feared that I would need to dig for many years in order to find enough evidence to justify the switch. My worries soon went from not finding enough to wondering if it all wasn't fitting together too easily. One day a graduate student in history, who was also conducting research at many of the same places in Chicago that I was, noticed that I was having great success. She told me that my research seemed like "shooting fish in a barrel." Oh, how lucky I was, she grinned. The whiteness of her skin and the blackness of her not-so-easy topic haunted me for days. While I was in a grocery store checkout line the next week, a white woman who looked as if she had been on her feet all day turned to me and complained about the Asian Indian woman in front of us. The Indian was paying with food stamps and arguing with the Latino clerk about an alleged overcharge. For a moment I was white, or perhaps just

"American," as the white woman treated me to a tirade about *them*. How would this fit into existing notions of the way lines were drawn in Chicago?, I wondered. There was a black, a white, an Asian, and a Latino. There were no Koreans involved, and I had two advanced degrees and an annual income of less than nine thousand dollars. The clerk was a man in a job held mostly by women. I realized that it was so easy to find evidence that challenged biracial-dependent explanations in the past because of how easily it could be done in the present.

Perhaps my research went so smoothly because of my own involvement with the student campaign for an Asian American studies program at Northwestern University. Three or four of the committee members would make their way up to Evanston almost every day during the weeks-long hunger strike. They gave money as well as their presence to the students' efforts. At one of the rallies held in support of the striking students, some of the student leaders encouraged me to take a turn at the microphone. As an African American graduate student, I had already shocked a few people by voicing support for the establishment of an Asian American undergraduate program.[12] Later on in the course of my fieldwork, one of the members told me that he remembered me from that rally. Whether that was the reason I was so easily accepted into the group is not clear. In the end, I was simply accepted, and there was no debate or questioning—at least not in my presence.

My grandmother, like many of my informants, led a life full of irony and contradictions about "fitting in" racially. My informants, like my grandmother, often grounded their thoughts in gender stereotypes and common sense that sometimes offended my sensibilities as a progressive woman and a child of the 1980s. My informants, however, like the ethnography I have constructed, continually question and challenge what it means to be raced in this world while recognizing that their lives have been shaped by a city and a country where race is wrongly defined in black and white. I write about them and use their words, thoughts, and actions admiringly because histories such as theirs have been hidden for much longer than the tapes and notes under my desk. This embarrassment of riches of tapes, notes, and archived material is a point of entry into ethnographic traditions—past and present.

CHAPTER THREE

Double-Crossing Chicago's Color Line

The Great Relocation of Japanese Americans in Postwar Race Ideology

Although it was not very extensive, Japanese American relocation to Chicago during and right after World War II is a significant factor in the history of race in America. Census figures show that the Japanese American population of Chicago increased from a little more than three hundred in 1940 to almost eleven thousand in 1950, but these figures likely underestimate the full magnitude of Japanese American migration to the city. Although precise figures are unavailable, it is estimated that as many as thirty thousand Japanese Americans passed through Chicago or lived there at some point during the 1940s. People may not talk about or point to it directly, but this movement of labor, which I call the great relocation, has become a linchpin in the falsely held idea that there is very little in common between Japanese and black Americans. The similarities between the two go unmentioned, as do the possible explanations for those similarities. Like the large migration of blacks to the North, the forced evacuation of Japanese Americans from the West Coast was about a group of "others" moving to Chicago because of a combination of politics and economics propelled by racism. The same shifts in labor and economics that had brought blacks to Chicago from sharecropping brought Japanese Americans from Internment camps to the black/white city, even if in lesser numbers. Both groups competed for jobs and housing as people of color in a city that was quickly losing its appetite for unskilled labor of any color. Even though Japanese Americans as a group were better educated than blacks and had more experience than blacks as business owners, both lived in a city where who employed you, how much you were paid, and where you could live were determined by the color of your nonwhite skin. But we have learned to downplay this history in favor of a view that the two groups have no common history and that Japanese Americans' relocation is of little importance to Chicago or U.S. race history.

For about twenty years after World War II, Chicago had the largest concentration of Japanese Americans in the country, but the government-approved and business-sponsored "great relocation" of Japanese Americans to Chicago has no Library of Congress subject heading. You will not find it in any index, and it is left out of most accounts of Japanese American history. There is no group of devoted scholars who have made their careers from theorizing about the impact of Japanese Americans moving to Chicago. But the mythology of the great relocation, that Japanese Americans arrived in the Midway Metropolis and thrived because of their particular cultural values, is at the heart of contemporary racial ideologies. According to the same mythology, Japanese Americans eventually left behind racism in Chicago, in other words being colored, by virtue of their superior family values and race culture.

During the 1940s and 1950s, the black/white narrative in Chicago was reinforced and recreated in part because of the relationship, imagined and real, between Japanese Americans and blacks. Japanese and black Americans came into daily contact in Chicago as workers, neighbors, and people of color, and there were varied opinions about what these encounters would mean for Japanese Americans and the articulation of race in the city. America's appetite for cultural, not material, explanations turned attentions away from what took place between Japanese Americans and blacks as each group struggled for political and economic equality. This study takes a closer look at the great relocation mythology and the ways that it reinforces our misconceptions about race while simultaneously providing ways for rethinking them. The key to reclaiming this forgotten element of Japanese American race history is the resurrection of the work of three Japanese American graduate students who, recognizing that the relocatees were still on the colored side of the color line, saw that they would face difficulties in their new home. These studies, besides providing rare accounts of how Japanese Americans were treated in those early years, shed light on Japanese Americans' varied opinions about their place in racialized Chicago. These accounts also suggest that when we say "race" in America, we should never forget that we are also talking about how we have come to misunderstand Japanese Americans in Chicago.

Brothers and Sisters Outsiders

On a typically "too hot for comfort" Chicago summer afternoon, I squinted into the microfilm reader in the Chicago Historical Society Library. As usual, my fellow researchers and the CHS staff busied themselves with genealogy research. Nothing seemed different from any other day. Telephone calls from out-of-towners about long-lost ancestors were answered, and white-haired men and women continued to gather materials for family records. But I will always remember that day. It was one of the few times when the self-consciousness I usually felt while researching at the library was absent. It wasn't that I had been unwelcome during my year of research there. It was more that I felt I didn't really belong there—and everybody knew it. The politics of archival research seemed all too painful most of the time. But on that particular day, I did not care that I was the lone black face in the building, except for the occasional janitor or security guard, for that is when I discovered Chicago according to Okada. The clickety-clack of fingers on the keyboards of laptops did not pound in my ears that day. I wore my pencils down to nubs with abandon. Who cared if eyebrows were raised when I asked for Japanese folders and files?

Okada's analysis (1947) of the arrival of Japanese American male workers into Chicago's World War II boom economy was the kind of record that I had never imagined existed. Okada organized his thesis around the differences faced by Japanese American men, skilled and unskilled, depending on the company they worked for and who their coworkers were. For Okada the differences between a unionized workplace and a nonunionized one were complicated by the color of coworkers, union officials, and bosses. One of Okada's most important findings was that Japanese Americans were treated one way when they were the only nonwhites in a nonunionized factory and a completely different way when they were workers in a multiracial unionized workplace. I was both shocked and thrilled by Okada's obsession with the importance of the relationships between Japanese Americans and blacks. I could not imagine who would have signed off on his thesis at the time. Okada saw Japanese Americans in a Chicago in which race did matter and not just in black and white. This was something that I imagined would ruffle

the papers and microfilms of my fellow Chicago Historical Society researchers. I had found a fellow outsider.

That evening, I rode my bicycle home in Chicago's notorious ninety-
degree summer heat. The entire bike ride was a blur. I rode up Lake
Shore Drive, past the high-rises for both the rich and the poor, past the
rehabbing that characterizes Chicago's North Side "neighborhoods in
transition." I didn't mind the bus exhaust, the giant potholes (there's
enough money to put up new Victorian-style retro street lamps, but
not enough to fix the massive canyons in the streets), or the honking
drivers who usually forced me into a combination wheeze-curse-hack. I
have proof, I have proof, I told myself. When I got home, my building's
Swedish American maintenance man and manager, Lorenz, waved and
smiled. We chatted about how hot it was. He helped me with my bicycle
up the stairs. I couldn't help thinking about how neither Okada nor I
could have lived in this Far North Side neighborhood in 1947.[1] I had a
flashback to the first time that I had met Lorenz, three years earlier. He
had been surprised to see the black body that went with what he must
have imagined was the white voice he had heard when I called about the
place. Back then he had been guarded. He had told me that he had nothing against renting to blacks, but that I should get my deposit and ap-
plication to the rental company as soon as possible, just in case. I have
never quite figured out how to explain the tone that was in his voice. It
was a strange mixture of concern and distaste. Although Lorenz had
not yet immigrated to the United States in 1947, I wondered what advice
he or his equivalent would have given to Dave Okada, the Japanese American graduate student. Would Okada have been considered a dubious
renter because of his color?

All that night I thought about Okada. I started mapping my plans to
find out as much as I could about him. Here was a study that acknowledged that Japanese Americans had arrived in Chicago during the war
and had lived and worked among whites (native-born Americans and
immigrants) and blacks. But it was also a study that had come out of
the University of Chicago Department of Sociology (UCDS) at its heyday. I had long ago learned to question most of the famous department's
most famous scholars because of their emphasis on race culture, the
notion of Chicago as a social laboratory, and "marginal man" theories
of race and ethnicity.[2] Even with all that Okada's study brought to light,
in the end, for Okada, it was that Japanese Americans' "culture" and

"attitudes toward work" were much better suited to economic success in Chicago than those of blacks. Even though Okada knew that Japanese Americans were affected by racism and discrimination in wartime Chicago and that their status in Chicago had a lot to do with how they were being compared with blacks, in the end he downplayed his findings because of what I imagine was his faith in the theories that made his department famous. That night I didn't know whether to laugh or to scream at "finding" Okada. How could I reconcile the fact that he was giving me the detail I wanted with the interpretations I distrusted?

On that second night I wondered how could I make sense of the two sides of Dave Okada's work. I believe that the answer is in his title: "Two Chicago Industrial Plants under Wartime Conditions." It was as if Okada did not want anyone to know that his research was about Japanese Americans, much less the ways that he was dealing with their shifting places in Chicago's racial hierarchies. It is probably not coincidence that I found Okada without knowing beforehand what I would find. Okada's work exists in a weird position exactly because it both challenged and supported the idea that race in America was a black culture thing. It was about Japanese Americans, but not really. It was about the material realities of racial discrimination, but not really. I think Okada is not considered important in race theory today because what he had to say is in direct conflict with what current race theory tells us to believe about race in Chicago and Japanese Americans' place within race theory. Okada was an outsider for sure.

Until those two hot summer days, I had never seen any of Okada's work mentioned anywhere else. I had been looking, but could only hope that work like his existed. Over the next few weeks, I learned that Okada had not been alone. There were at least two other Japanese American graduate students whose degrees resulted from their research about those early years of Japanese American history, and other than their dissertations on microfilm, there wasn't much more to find out about them. They had become invisible to scholars who wrote about race, Japanese American history, or even UCDS intellectual history. As "insider researchers," Dave Okada, Eugene Uyeki, and Evelyn Setsuko Nishi were part of a Chicago School tradition of nonwhites trained to research their own "people."[3] But as "Orientals" in an institution where the "Negro problem" was at the time becoming the focal point of studies about race and urban issues, they were outsiders.

Yet even these outsiders were very different from each other. The three studies had different focuses—Okada's was Japanese workers' treatment in wartime factories, Uyeki's was the post-relocation psychology of Nisei in Chicago, and Nishi's was the ultimate triumph of Japanese American community values over adversity. But no matter how they approached the newly arriving Japanese Americans' experiences in Chicago, there can be no mistake that they were well aware of the relationship between Japanese Americans' fate in Chicago and that of the other outsider/colored group—blacks.

When They Were Colored

One of the most important ways that race in Chicago openly played out in the years during and right after World War II was in a quiet but bitter battle over just how "colored" Japanese American relocatees were. The question of how they would fare in the workplace or as neighbors was constantly being reworked and reconfigured in those early years. But the comparisons of Japanese Americans' problems with those of blacks did not begin in Chicago. As early as 1924, Robert Park, the granddaddy of race relations theory, had written that the "Oriental" and the "Negro" problems were the same in origin and solution. Park was confident that both groups' problems would go away with time. Of course, for Park, who dedicated his life to the belief that cultural assimilation was the primary means of economic success, this was inevitable. Given his life history, Park's interest in Negroes and Orientals is not difficult to understand. Park arrived at the University of Chicago Department of Sociology from Tuskegee Institute, where he had been Booker T. Washington's ghostwriter and friend. He conducted a landmark study of California race relations on the Pacific Coast in the 1920s. While there, he became "enchanted" with Japanese culture. As visiting professor at the University of Hawaii from 1931 to 1933, Park renewed his fascination with Japanese and Chinese immigrant culture. But even as Park spent most of his life among Asians and blacks and made scattered statements implying that he felt the two groups shared a similar existence in the United States, neither he nor any of his students ever attempted to study the groups in tandem. If only he had stayed at the UCDS a while longer. By the time Okada, Uyeki, and Nishi arrived at the UCDS during the 1940s, Park had retired. By then the UCDS had come under the direction of Everett Hughes and Louis Wirth. Each of them claimed to be Park's rightful heir, even though they disagreed on how to best approach the "Negro problem," which by that time was quickly becoming the urban problem. Park's ideas about cultural similarities between Orientals and Negroes seemed lost to those who followed him. But for reasons that are not entirely clear and that probably had some connection to the War Relocation Authority (WRA) funding of research on the relocation, the three Japanese American graduate students gave Park's speculation about the linkages between Orientals and Negroes a final spin.[4] Through the eyes of Japanese American graduate students, one a master's student and the others doctoral students, Robert Park's ideas about the Oriental and Negro problems came to life. The students paid attention to how Japanese Americans fit into Chicago as coworkers, employees, and neighbors by highlighting what they assumed was traditional Japanese culture. In each case they would have made Park, who died in 1944 and thus never even knew of their existence, proud.

Okada and Uyeki both tell us that Japanese Americans experienced daily lives that brought them in contact with blacks and that there was some disagreement about how to interpret their connections to blacks during the early years of relocation. Some, like those in Okada's factory studies, were vehemently opposed to being compared with blacks. Others, like those Uyeki interviewed, were unsure as to how close or how far away they were from being colored—as well as what to do about it. From Okada and Uyeki, we learn that Japanese Americans were aware of the fact that in Chicago they were colored, or at least nonwhite. We also learn from their research that many Japanese Americans were unhappy with being on the colored side of the racial divide in Chicago. But besides giving some of the only accounts of how Japanese Americans thought about their racial positions in Chicago, Okada and Uyeki give us proof that Japanese Americans and blacks in Chicago, at least in the beginning, were on the same side of a shifting color line.

Perhaps one of the most intense moments in Japanese American history in Chicago was a strike that took place in 1944. The challenges that Japanese Americans posed to racism as usual in Chicago are illustrated well in what happened between Japanese Americans and whites. Interestingly enough, this was one of the two small factories that Okada researched where Japanese Americans, not blacks, were the only nonwhite employees. Okada relates that, throughout a CIO-supported strike in

December at Company "B," Japanese American rank and file were asked by white union officials not to walk picket lines. The factory employed only a hundred workers, thirty-one of whom were Nisei between the ages of twenty-one and thirty. The majority of the white workers were older and had less education than their Japanese American coworkers. But no matter how small the numbers, what took place during the strike is eye-opening. Japanese Americans were told by the officials that their appearance in newspaper photos might jeopardize public sympathy for the strikers during a time of war with Japan. Okada believed that many of the Japanese Americans had been ambivalent about joining the union in the first place, but had done so because they thought it was the right thing to do if they wanted to avoid causing trouble. If this was true, the Nisei workers might have preferred not to walk the picket lines. In fact, if Okada's suspicions are right, a good number may not have even cared about the strike, since many of the Nisei had come from business-owning families on the West Coast and might have sided with management had they been back home. The request to lie low during the strike is by itself proof that Chicago's labor history should not focus strictly on black and white. Yet there is something more that Okada can tell us about the often unbelievable aspects of the lines that were drawn between and among Chicagoans.

Sometime in the middle of the strike a meeting was called by union officials. Officials wanted to make clear that part of their demands to management were for the hiring of more colored workers. An upset and vocal group of white workers challenged union leaders. According to Okada's sources, the meeting was antagonistic, and fiery words were exchanged between the group of angry white workers and the white union officials. But what took place after this meeting may be one of the best examples of the battles about what exactly Japanese Americans "were." The group of white protesters pulled some of the Nisei aside to tell them, "[Y]ou fellows, you're not colored—you're white" (Okada 1947: 81). The threat of unionization in wartime factories, the fear of black workers in segregated workplaces, and Japanese Americans relocating to Chicago as overqualified and overeducated hourly laborers are just a few of the factors behind the way relocatees experienced race in Chicago.

Okada quotes an informant as saying, "[T]he reason the company hired us is because they didn't have any choice." He continues: "We Nisei can't expect much more right now. The good jobs in good places are going to guys who don't look like Japs, even the *kurombos [sic]* (Negroes) have a better chance to get in" (Okada 1947: 68). Another man described his attitude while at work: "I don't hold back. No use being timid. The other night, the foreman tried to hurry me up, but I told him to go to hell. I asked him, 'Is this a slave or a free state?'" (70). Some of Okada's informants described being shunned on Chicago's trains and buses by whites and compared their treatment to that received by blacks on public transport. Clearly these men were aware that the world they lived in was neither Japanese/white nor black/white and that their positions in it bore a closer resemblance to the black side than the white side. Whether indignant over being considered by employers as lower than "even *kurombos*" or invoking slavery to a white manager to express dissatisfaction, Japanese Americans were well aware that their lives were connected to blacks. But male relocatees' opinions about whether or not these similarities were good or bad were diverse.

Almost ten years after Okada's work, Uyeki's depiction (1953) of Chicago's Japanese American community portrays a group that was just beginning to move away from the "colored" side of the color line. For Uyeki, Nisei in particular wanted to assimilate into Chicago and seemed to see a need to give their children an opportunity to become "regular" Americans—or in the words of my informant Dan Hayashi, "American means white to Japanese Americans and everybody else, too." But even with his focus on the psychology behind Japanese American behavior, Uyeki made it clear that Japanese Americans came into contact every day with many different racial groups of coworkers and neighbors, especially blacks. This contact meant active choices made by the Japanese Americans to decide how to act upon this daily contact—which to Uyeki was a natural thing, and wanting to assimilate would mean choosing to sever any connections to blacks whatsoever. Even in Uyeki's classically Chicago School chapter on Nisei attitudes toward intermarriage, he makes it clear that many of the people he interviewed might reluctantly accept a Chinese, Jewish, or Mexican son- or daughter-in-law, but a Negro in-law would be a serious problem. When the majority of Japanese Americans in Chicago in the 1950s could still not afford to do the things necessary to make sure that their children would become "American," like moving to white neighborhoods, the desire to leave their coloredness behind, in Uyeki's opinion, weighed heavily on them.

In the Twilight Zone

Even though Uyeki concluded that "the Nisei realize that if they should undertake to identify any closer with the Negroes, their own status position would be endangered," he made sure to point out that not everybody thought that way (Uyeki 1953: 148). One of Uyeki's informants, an accountant, stated: "The Sanseis...are going to occupy a position in the twilight zone between the blacks and whites. The problem between the blacks and the whites is a great one—more than many people realize. I think we have a grand chance to do something" (147). Regardless of what view Japanese Americans had about the "Negro question" in relation to the "Nikkei question," the fact was that Uyeki and his informants saw Chicago as a city that wasn't rigidly about blacks and whites and their place in it.

Not even Nishi—whose account (1963) of Japanese Americans in Chicago reads like the kind of race pride/cultural nationalism that Louis Farrakhan or Marcus Garvey might have written for blacks—could deny that Japanese Americans were highly aware of their position in Chicago in relation to blacks.[5] The only time Nishi ever directly mentions blacks in her work is when she describes Japanese American community leaders, in the early years of relocation and in their efforts to set up social agencies especially for relocatees, calling upon a prominent black leader for help in getting monetary assistance from Chicago social welfare agencies. Nishi explains that over the course of a few months, Japanese American community leaders followed the advice of the black leader and eventually asked for money from the agencies, even though in Nishi's opinion this went against Japanese traditions of receiving "handouts" from outsiders. She speculates that this request for money was not the correct choice for the leaders, because white social service agency officials denied their requests. The leaders were told that "special pleading" would not be tolerated from Japanese Americans. The system had spoken and the Japanese American leaders listened.

In Nishi's framework, which I will discuss further in the next section, this moment in Japanese American history in Chicago is an example of Japanese traditions of self-sufficiency explaining why Japanese Americans, by the early 1960s (when she finished her dissertation), had left their coloredness behind. But even so, she speculated that when Japanese Americans had once asked for help from blacks, blacks had eagerly come to their assistance because of a shared distrust of whites. Nishi imagined that acknowledging and springboarding from these shared experiences might help in "bridging the schism between the dominant and minority groups.... [T]he emerging definition of means for the goal of integration called for a concerted drive to organize the afflicted" (Nishi 1963: 247). Yes, even Nishi observed that the Japanese and black citizens of Chicago faced the world in similar ways, even if in the end Japanese cultural traditions were superior, in her view.

I offer another possible explanation that may romanticize this moment as resistance, but that could have been true as well. What if the groups were not trying to bridge gaps between mainstream and afflicted, but instead between colored and colored? Could it have been that the Nisei/ Negro elite leaders' meetings and efforts to get funding for Japanese Americans in Chicago were blatant attempts by both groups to "get over" on the system that mandated competition between colored community leaders over the title of most deserving "problem race"? In either case, Nishi knew there was no way to understand Japanese Americans in Chicago without detailing the relationships between Japanese American and black leaders and how they were affected by the whites who controlled Chicago's social welfare agencies.

Comparisons between Japanese Americans and blacks were as critical to "race in Chicago" during those years as they are today. Only now the comparisons seem to have become more mean-spirited, perhaps because the jobs are even fewer and the gaps between us all are widening. The competition for a comfortable existence in the late twentieth century and competition for "best minority group" made the lines among people of color more divisive than ever. The impression remains that Japanese Americans never thought about or realized that they were not completely welcome in a place like Chicago, with a reputation for racism against blacks.

Americans' conceptions of the politics and economics surrounding race have always been a puzzling mix of yarns and daily experiences. But Okada, Uyeki, and Nishi represent what happened as the lines that intersected Japanese Americans and blacks shifted and continued to affect how Japanese Americans saw themselves and how Chicago classified them. There is no way to point fingers at certain individuals or groups who reconfigured the lines. But what happened was neither a natural outcome nor inevitable. The convergence of theoretical and political trends going on in postwar Chicago and America meant that the divisions between the groups became extremely important to the resolution of postwar race problems. Most of all, it seems to me that Okada, Uyeki, and Nishi were trying to understand and predict how Japanese Americans would fare in a post-Internment America. The three knew that Japanese Americans were being compared, from the minute they began to arrive in the early 1940s, with blacks. They knew, perhaps better than any others at the time, that Japanese American relocatees would have to contend with the Negro problem in Chicago. So even as they focused on the cultural assimilation process for relocatees, as would be expected of Chicago School students, they devoted much of their analysis to Japanese American/Negro relations. This meant paying strict attention to the race-related problems that both groups faced together. So when talking about the hiring practices of Chicago's wartime industries or how Japanese American leaders dealt with the city's white-run social welfare agencies, the three researchers wrote about blacks, too. They tell us, by giving example after example, that everyday life in Chicago right after the war was not a natural process of assimilation. They show us that Japanese Americans' relocation to Chicago instead caused a great deal of questioning by the researchers and the people whom they studied. They give us a way to see that over fifteen short years there was no smooth or natural transition for Japanese Americans from colored to "model."

The students' work marks specific points when Americans began to accept race in Chicago as black, while at the same time embracing the postwar ideology that inequality was due to inherited cultures and behaviors. The three knew that the color line was not stationary and that the presence of Japanese Americans in Chicago mocked its binarity, with or without culture in the picture. They took notice of the Japanese American/black connection because Japanese Americans and blacks in Chicago had been placed in competition with each other, and Japanese Americans knew it. The three point to the reasons it was so important, to those whose fortunes (and academic careers) were being made from working-class people of color, to keep the two groups as far apart as possible. During a time when Chicago was undergoing major economic and political changes brought on by the war mobilization, a Japanese American/black coalition, even if only among the more well-off members of both groups, would surely have meant a different notion of race in Chicago today. And later, as calls for civil and economic equality from blacks and other groups threatened to upset America's race/political/economic systems, the idea that race culture explains class position might have died, if not for the convenience that allowed "America" to hold up Japanese Americans as models to blacks and other people of color. I argue that this modern-day assumption sprang from the days when Japanese Americans were colored. The three students recognized and pointed to the importance of understanding the links that fused Japanese Americans and blacks in Chicago.

The students are absent from our contemporary understandings of both Japanese American history and race theory, although they have explicitly influenced the direction of both fields of inquiry. The neglect of Uyeki et al. is a serious problem, but also an example of the powerful hold of the black/white color line on race theory. These works speak to understandings of the color line, race history in Chicago, labor history, and the intellectual history of the social sciences. By ignoring them, we can collectively ignore the interweaving of Japanese Americans and blacks into American conceptions of race and race culture and the apparent ability of some groups to leave coloredness behind.

Predictors of Success

Despite seeming to be more aware than his contemporaries or the majority of Americans today, Robert Park was influential in creating the view of race and culture that is behind contemporary stereotyped images of Asians and blacks. By stressing culture in "American race relations," Park helped to create an environment in which culture was thought to be the reason that Orientals and Negroes faced similar problems assimilating in 1924. It was not a web of racism but culture that helped to define Orientals and Negroes as problems in American society. And it was cultural assimilation that would take them from problem to successful "Americans." Today Americans accept cultural poverty, dependency, social psychology, and family values as scientific explanations for the problems that now belong to blacks. Racialized cultural practices continue to be seen as a predictor of success. Easier for us to blame it on upbringing or bad lifestyle choices than to acknowledge the politics and economics of "divide and conquer" racism. We swallow it all today because of Park's influence—not in spite of it.

Irony is one of those rhetorical tricks that is easily confused or misused. It is often difficult to describe it without using an example. English instructors devise ingenious tricks to teach the concept to their students. One professor has used a comic-book example in his freshman classes. Although it is not really the stuff textbooks are made of, Superman's vulnerability to kryptonite is indeed ironic. The rock is harmless to mere men while it cripples and sickens the man of steel. It is exactly this combination of unexpected and almost unbelievable contradiction that is at the root of irony. It is also at the center of the ways that Japanese Americans have been fitted into American race theory and Chicago race politics over the past fifty years.

Unexpectedly and unbelievably—ironically—the University of Chicago Department of Sociology produced three studies of Japanese American relocation to Chicago during World War II that challenge our view of race in Chicago and about Japanese Americans' place in race theory. Yet there is no way that Okada, Uyeki, and Nishi could have escaped their roots, even if they had wanted to. They were surrounded by researchers asking about the effects of World War II on race relations in the urban north. These were researchers who sought their answers strictly in terms of the lines between black and white and the process of cultural assimilation. Works like *Black Metropolis* (Drake and Cayton [1945] 1993) and *The Negro Family in Chicago* (Frazier 1932) were the department's standard. The three graduate students might have come to the department at different times, but their surroundings influenced them for sure. Sharing hallways and conference rooms with colleagues and mentors who today form the backbone of today's black and culture-centric American race theory, the three, like all researchers, predictably reflect their intellectual heritage.[6] All three quoted the better-known UCDS studies throughout their own work when they asserted that Negroes faced the world culturally unprepared for life's demands while Japanese relocatees had the kind of culture and family life that would allow them to succeed in Chicago.

That seems fitting, since most of what Americans misunderstand about race in the United States has roots in the golden age of UCDS sociology. Why do our collective thoughts about race, politics, and economics always come down to discussions of morality or cultural differences? The Chicago School taught us to think of Chicago and the people who lived in it as examples of how race, cultural assimilation, and the "American Dream" worked in the twentieth century. The work gave us the imagery of the immigrant whose children, once thoroughly Americanized in culture and work ethic, worked their way up to the middle class. UCDS theories about the Back of the Yards and the Black Metropolis made Chicago famous. Or was it the other way around? In either case, sometime around the early sixties, race, Chicago, and culture—due in part to the popularity of the Chicago School findings in places like the U.S. Congress—became our holy trinity, which is invoked whenever we want to understand or rectify America's "urban issues." Today the legacy of culture as predictor of success is strong, as terms like "culture of poverty" dance around in our heads and spew from our politicians' mouths with ease.

Just like kryptonite, the three studies support the principles of the UCDS that continue to misguide us today—culture first and economics second, with a good dose of seeing race in that persistent black/white dichotomy—but that also pack a powerful and decisive punch to any current misconceptions that Japanese Americans just "slid" into Chicago or that theorizing about similarities between Oriental and Negro problems in America ended when Park died. Their contribution to the UCDS view of race culture—that Japanese American culture is formulated as family, psychology, and community—must be reckoned with by today's researchers. Nishi is especially useful in this regard, because her work was clearly influenced by a political atmosphere in which America's racism was beginning to crumble, as nonwhites, youth, and women were pushing the established lines of inequality. But it was also a time when conservative and moderate leaders were searching for answers.

The picture that Nishi paints, of Japanese American culture as proof of Japanese Americans' seemingly successful relocation in Chicago, may have been an image too convenient to pass up for those who wanted to press for patience and passivity. Whatever Nishi's political views, her study reveals that culture as the explanation for Japanese Americans no longer being seen as colored in Chicago is the unspoken assumption behind what we mean when we say "race" in America.

By 1963, when Evelyn Nishi defended her dissertation, the Japanese American question in Chicago had become moot as well as muted. Nishi represented the wave of the future of Japanese American scholarship with her view that Japanese Americans had never been nor ever would be interested in being "colored." In Nishi's account of what had happened since the end of the war, the relatively small Japanese American community had overcome the stigma of Internment and relocation by the sheer power of cultural values and traditions. According to Nishi, there was unlimited proof that the growing Japanese American community in Chicago had triumphed over discrimination. From the discrimination faced in finding places for the living and the dead—housing and burial plots—to intergenerational fighting among Issei and Nisei community leaders, Japanese Americans had survived and prospered by tapping into their strong family values and silent perseverance. She determined that Japanese Americans had almost been on the brink of relocation ruin in Chicago, with an early explosion of unwed mothers and juvenile delinquency. But self-determination and the use of community policing of those who might have strayed had done their job, not help from the government or loud protests. Japanese Americans in Chicago had overcome the worst—in other words avoided becoming colored—by allowing the natural process of assimilation to work for them. Nishi gave no figures to support her claims that Japanese Americans had "made it" and mainly relied upon her intimate knowledge (her father was a prominent Issei leader in the early years of the relocation) of Issei/Nisei tensions. But Nishi used that insider information, and combined it with her Chicago School training, to argue that Japanese values were just like those of the upwardly mobile interaction patterns of the larger society. In other words, Japanese Americans were more like whites than members of "lesser society."

Nishi's work was clearly rooted in the relatively new belief at the time that Japanese Americans shared little with colored groups in Chicago. Her work may be one of the earliest examples of the usefulness of "model minority" rhetoric, which came into fashion by the 1980s, to those who were interested in keeping race a black issue. Nishi, of course, is not responsible for the Asian American model minority mythology. But her early version of it tells us that the notion of color and culture in Chicago and the role of Japanese Americans and blacks played an important, if not primary, role in its creation. She acknowledged that relocation had been a horrible occurrence that had a lot to do with race prejudice. But it wasn't just that the natural process of cultural assimilation, the Chicago School legacy to postwar race theory, had worked for Japanese Americans. The great relocation mythology became important to race theory, as it was developing in its present incarnation, for another reason. Japanese Americans had been racially discriminated against in one of America's most racially charged cities—Chicago School theories had helped to establish that characterization as fact—and had made it across the success line via their humble cultural values.

Although there were no outright comparisons with blacks, it was not difficult to see how Nishi's work was both a response and an answer to the question, "Why are the Japanese successful?" In her work Japanese Americans had overcome racial stigma. Japanese Americans were the counterexample to those, in this case blacks, who said that the system was not fair to people of color. It was more than just being patient—something that the Chicago School studies almost always seemed to advocate.[7]

In retrospect it seems obvious that Nishi's work was written as a direct answer and protest to the calls for integration and the militancy that frightened many Americans. Her use of Japanese American success in Chicago to argue the ability to make it in racist Chicago marks a turning point in Japanese American/black history and race theory in general. But it is even more striking because this was only twenty years after Okada and Uyeki had openly described undeniably tension-filled relationships between Japanese Americans and blacks.

This idea about integration demands closer attention. Nishi writes about the word "integration" as an "emotion-laden term" for Japanese Americans because of the pain of Internment and resettlement. Japanese American community leaders in Chicago "sought to give 'integration' a different meaning, now on the level of *personal* adjustment, about which the Japanese American collectivity was obligated to take *responsibility*" (italics mine) (Nishi 1963: 202). By taking the word "integration" and placing it into the Japanese American context of Internment and relocation, Nishi was able to imply that integration was a misguided process because of what it had done to Japanese Americans. The federal government had forced "integration" on Japanese Americans, and it had almost ruined Japanese American cultural traditions. There was a lesson to be learned from the Japanese American experience. Any group who called for integration was calling for a disruption of natural processes; Japanese Americans were proof of that. Integration was better thought to be about personal responsibility and not government intervention. "The social structural connection between values of culture and the personalities of the members" was at the root of Japanese American success (12). The relationship between culture and success couldn't have been made any clearer: not only are culture and morality at the heart of why people are poor, but federal intervention (affirmative action) does more harm than good. Nishi's work, intentionally or not, is a vital study in understanding the roots of the theoretical place we are in today.

Unlike Okada and Uyeki, who openly wrote about the link between the images and realities of Japanese Americans and blacks in 1940s Chicago, Nishi wrote about the same periods of time with a 1960s research sensibility. Nishi's work has none of Okada's and Uyeki's uncertainty about whether it was "the system" or culture that predicted success. Nishi did not pay attention to the many different factors that Okada and Uyeki wrote about, even if only a little, factors in Japanese American relocatees' greater ability to "fit" into Chicago than blacks. Today it is unclear how much of any of this was due to intellectual differences among the three. After all, there is no law that says Japanese American scholars must have a unified view of the same situations. But what jumps out when I compare the three, keeping in mind the contexts in which they wrote, is that Nishi's work represents a marked change in how the Japanese American/ black relationship was interpreted. In postwar Chicago, Japanese Americans who had left Internment camps, graduated from college, or returned from war service lived and worked within a system of race and ethnic culture, neighborhood, and employment that had long interested University of Chicago sociologists. Japanese Americans' efforts to recreate their lives in a segregated city with a history of racial tensions between blacks and whites provided graduate student "native researchers" with marvelous opportunities to tell us part of an untold history.

It was as if all three were tormented by struggles, intellectual and personal, to prove that Japanese Americans, by virtue of their culture, should not be considered "colored." And so they wrote about what they saw as a united Japanese American community based on respect for elders and conformity. They wrote about ancient traditions brought over from Japan and then concluded that blacks in Chicago were discriminated against because they had no inherited traditions. By doing so they were reflecting and participating in what was becoming the scholarly and popular view of Japanese Americans in postwar America. Japanese Americans had the skills and cultural traditions to work their way across the color line and blacks did not. They did all of this even if that meant that they would have to ignore the troubles that Japanese Americans were having in Chicago and put more emphasis on the "positive" moves toward assimilation. They closed their minds to the many instances of

Japanese Americans imagining themselves closer to blacks than to whites. They had little choice, given their intellectual training. As Japanese Americans studying Japanese Americans in a department and a city that was used to dealing with race as a black and white issue, the three seemed to be praying for the time when the promises of the Chicago School would come true. They used blacks as the litmus test to see how and when race would decline in significance for Japanese Americans.

Even if their ideas were well intentioned, they tell us to believe that culture and personal behavior, not racism and discrimination, kept blacks down and allowed Japanese Americans up. Although they never once suggested it in their finished projects, part of what these three researchers were doing was explaining or trying to understand what they saw as the decreasing Oriental and the increasing Negro components of American race theory. But by relying on culture as an explanation, they ignored the many other explanations that their research suggested. At the same time they also showed us the other side, or rather what remains unspoken when we assume that Japanese Americans are model minorities. We can begin to imagine what is behind the commonly held assumptions that Japanese Americans have made it and no longer are central to the way race works in America. They show us that in just twenty years, there was a change in the perception of the connections between blacks and Japanese Americans in Chicago. They went from being seen as "colored" problems to being viewed as examples of culture as a predictor of success in racist Chicago. Nikkei in Chicago were the proof that cultural change, not structural change, was the key to minority success. As Chicago's and America's political and economic needs changed, so did the theories about Japanese Americans' place in Chicago. As industries' needs for unskilled labor continued to decline in the years following World War II and blacks' calls for an end to discrimination rose, explanations about Japanese Americans' postwar success in Chicago gained in popularity. More specifically, the belief that Japanese American cultural traditions explained what seemed to be wide-scale relocation accomplishments in Chicago became extremely important to keeping everyone and everything in its proper place and perspective.

Today Japanese Americans have become models—model minorities who, even during the redress movement of the 1980s, appear to be the paragons of middle-class American values. It would seem that Japanese Americans have made it—economically and racially. But even if this is true, it has come at a cost. That is what the three studies scream out at us, even if unwillingly. The beginnings of both the mythology of Asian Americans as model minorities and the ideology that blackness defines race in America are there in the three texts. And by the early 1960s, scholarly analysis of Japanese Americans' relocation to Chicago had become a perfect component of the idea that morality and culture were at the root of ethnic identity and success or failure. Gone were the earlier models that tried to understand how Japanese Americans were symbolically and materially tied to blacks in Chicago. In their place were the models that we use today. The history of Japanese Americans in Chicago, up from relocation, was proof for many that race in America and in Chicago was a black thing after all. The battle was over.

The Great Relocation

Comparison is seldom, if ever, made between the federal government's efforts to relocate Japanese Americans to Chicago and the larger and much longer migration of blacks to Chicago. Today race scholars apply the term "great migration" to different waves of black migrants. The term and the movement are considered key factors in understanding Chicago's race and labor histories. Unlike the case with nonexistent great relocation studies, results of a keyword search on the term "great migration" would be hard to manage. The number of books and articles, not to mention the wide range of thoughts they represent, would confirm what race scholars today already know. The movement of thousands of blacks to northern cities from the South between World War I and World War II is a defining element of U.S. race history. But even with multiple perspectives on twentieth-century shifts in capital and labor or the changes in local or regional politics that go along with great migration theories, the focus has remained on blacks. There is never any mention of the great relocation of Japanese Americans to Chicago.[8]

The migrations of more than 1.3 million blacks "up" from Down South to Chicago's workplaces and neighborhoods were powerful events in U.S. history that cannot be denied or deemphasized. Whether forced or lured out of the South, black men and women migrating north changed the realities of everyday life anywhere they moved. In Chicago in particular this was especially true. But the same could be said about Japanese Americans who moved to Chicago. True, Japanese Americans came in smaller numbers than blacks, but the peak of their migration in 1945 was around the time when black men and women were still making their way up from the Deep South to northern cities. Even with these points of intersection, the two groups' migrations have never been overtly compared.

The relocation of Japanese Americans suggests by implied fictions that Japanese Americans made it in Chicago; however, the great relocation, as I use the term, tells another story. We must address the differences and similarities between the Japanese American and the black migrations, and the two groups' experiences of discrimination in housing and employment, when trying to understand race in Chicago.

By accepting the great migration as the defining element of theories about race in Chicago, scholars of race have slighted or ignored the entry of Japanese Americans into postwar Chicago, even allowing for the differences in numbers. But that movement of Japanese Americans is part of an enormously complex history. For most Americans, the relocation of Japanese Americans to Chicago does not seem as important as the movement of blacks to Chicago. Even though the former group is excluded from mainstream race theory, the great relocation, and the mythology that surrounds it, is essential to understanding how foolishly we cling to our present race ideologies. The great migration has inaccurately become postwar race theory's poster child, both because and in spite of the great relocation's place in Chicago's history.

If emphasizing the great relocation seems like a feeble attempt to reconcile Japanese Americans into a black-centric definition of race in Chicago, that is not the case. What I want to underscore is that we continue to use the black movement as the only movement of raced labor that matters and thus ignore the possibilities that movements like the great relocation provide for understanding U.S. labor history. Instead of noting that similar forces brought both groups to Chicago or that people in both groups made individual choices about their lives based on the ways race and place played out in Chicago's factories, social welfare agencies, and research institutions, we lose perspective. We don't even bother to ask whether and how governments, businesses, and academics have taken active roles in creating and maintaining our experience and images of race.

The catch is that being out of sight doesn't necessarily mean being out of mind. The great relocation is unspoken today, but since World War II it has become an integral part of the mythology that race in Chicago equals "black in Chicago." By adding "great" to the relocation of Japanese Americans, I have given a fanciful title to what I see as an important part of today's assumptions about race. But really, I haven't done anything more than to point to an event that is already an inconspicuous part of the presumptions that great migration theories make.

This is not to argue that Japanese Americans had it just as bad as, or even worse than, blacks when they moved to Chicago. In fact, an important difference between the two populations' movements is that Japanese Americans arrived in Chicago with economic and organizational support from the WRA, a federal agency. Most blacks had little or no support from the government. But Japanese Americans were enticed out of Internment camps by many of Chicago's biggest nondefense industries. Instead of the federal government as the middleman, blacks had middlemen agents to bring them North to meet Chicago's demand for labor. The arrival of Japanese Americans definitely did not cause the division between black and white to become fiercer, or even more important. But the great relocation helped to make it more fragile by challenging the premises upon which "race as we know it" were based. With the protection and legitimacy that well-accepted great migration theories provide, we can imagine that Japanese Americans have left race behind. In reality, today's race theory has tried unsuccessfully to leave them behind.

The great relocation is a powerful mythology in U.S. race theory. It is powerful because in reality, Japanese Americans' relocation to Chicago was difficult and even more difficult to forget. They were relocating to places like Chicago, Detroit, and Cleveland because of some of the most serious violations of civil rights that have ever taken place in the United States.[9] But even before being rounded up and cordoned off, Japanese Americans had experienced a variety of brands of U.S. racism. Long before finding themselves in Chicago, Japanese Americans of first, second, and third generations knew to varying degrees that racism wasn't just about blacks. The discrimination that Japanese Americans had experienced on the West Coast and in Internment camps was replaced with a new version once they began to relocate outside of the Pacific Coast. Those who went to live in Chicago learned how to deal with Chicago-style discrimination while also experiencing a new kind of freedom that came with no longer being the primary focus of racism fueled by economics.[10] The Internment, as well as the relocation to which it gave birth, is as ironic in Japanese American history as racism in the Deep

South and the great migration were in black American history. But because of the mythology that goes along with the great relocation, none of us look at these similarities and see them for what they are. Behind every good tale, there is some truth. Japanese Americans and blacks shared many of the same experiences of wartime discrimination. But at the same time both groups experienced for the first time opportunities that were just a little bit better—or even in some cases a whole lot better—than those they'd known previously. This is the truth behind the mythology. But what makes the great relocation really stand out as crafted lore is that in contemporary race theory, the similarities between Japanese American and black migrations to Chicago are recognized only in order to draw stark lines between the two groups.

I keep raising the point that Japanese Americans' place in racial theory is both hidden and visible. But mainly I have been drawing attention to the idea of Japanese Americans in Chicago over the past fifty years as obscurely invaluable to contemporary race theories, especially those that deal with the great migration. The Chicago version of the "GR" mythology says that Japanese Americans left Internment camps, colleges, or wartime battlefields to find better lives in Chicago. It continues by pointing out that Japanese Americans were placed into competition with blacks and "beige" whites for jobs and housing. Although Japanese Americans had a higher level of education and job skills than most of their competitors, they were also "Japanese" during a war with Japan, so clearly they were able to overcome discrimination. The mythology concludes with images of today. Japanese Americans in Chicago have indeed become honorary whites and are most concerned about keeping their strong family values intact despite a high rate of third- and fourth-generation out-marriage.[11] There is no need to explain, in the "open" version of Japanese Americans' relocation story. Americans are wonderful learners. The great relocation in mythology and not reality, from beginning to end, supports the idea that race was and is a black problem. The great relocation, as opposed to the reality of Japanese Americans' migration to Chicago during a politically and economically charged time period, allows Japanese Americans to be factored out of race theory. It makes their experiences and how they were related to blacks and other people of color seem irrelevant. Worst of all, it supports the corollary of great migration theory that is the most deceitful and the oldest: Culture and morality explain the class differences among "races" that we see today.

By implying that Japanese Americans made a smooth transition to Chicago, the great relocation myth allows researchers to cling to the idea that the Japanese are different. The result has been that most Chicagoans, and this seems to include Japanese Americans and blacks as well, have no idea how the two migrations correspond to each other. While the relocation of Japanese Americans to Chicago on a large scale was an opportunity for the federal government to try to right a racist wrong, it brought them to a city where they would ultimately be compared with blacks. Japanese Americans' relative success in Chicago compared with blacks' relative failure made them the living proof that any "bad hand" that a racial group might be dealt could be overcome. No one seems to pay attention to the changes going on in hiring and housing patterns in a city where race and class were undergoing major reworkings because of the very shifts in population that were encouraging Chicago's growth. Thanks to the quiet factoring of Japanese Americans' relocation into Chicago race theory, "up from slavery" has been met with "up from Internment." How great relocation mythology affects Japanese Americans who have not lived up to it will be examined in a later chapter. But for now it is enough to realize that none of what happened between the arrival of Japanese Americans in Chicago in the 1940s and their "disappearance" from the colored side around the 1960s was smooth, nor was it due to some innate or superior Japanese culture. What Okada, Uyeki, and Nishi detail most clearly is that the great migration mythology doesn't tell the whole multilayered story of what happened when Japanese Americans joined blacks in Chicago.

The three UCDS Japanese American graduate students mark the thin lines between the past and the present that the "great" mythologies hide. For the twenty years between the time they began to defend their work and the time it was tucked away on microfilm, the question of Japanese American relocatees' success was never settled. There was still hope, as seen in the three studies and the situations that they describe, that Japanese Americans could start anew in the Midwest. Those studies read like many of the great migration narratives that exist today. And though it may seem like semantic trickery to present the great relocation as a challenge to the great migration's hold on race theory, I want to open up the wound that the three also helped to hastily close in those early postwar years. We continue to suffer theoretically from the damage of rigidly drawing the color line between blacks and everyone else. Despite the mythology, Japanese Americans did not and have not crossed the race barrier. We cannot fully understand the connection between the great relocation and today's ideas about race without paying homage to the house that culture built, where the great relocation narrative has its roots—the University of Chicago Department of Sociology.

I do not think that Okada, Uyeki, and Nishi should be labeled as racists. In fact they looked at race politics in Chicago with an awareness that was more sophisticated than that of most of their contemporaries. It is not because they are not white that I see them this way. The three, all Japanese American relocatees themselves, were trying to find their place in Chicago. U.S. history is filled with examples of people of color, using whatever means available, attempting to differentiate themselves from whatever group of color was at the bottom of the pile at that particular moment. Often the group at the bottom was black, but not always.[12] No, the three weren't racists. They knew that the relationships, assumed and actual, between blacks and Japanese Americans in Chicago would have to be made starkly clear by researchers if any of us were going to understand how race worked. What was sad was their conclusion that, if the color line was to be a division between black and white, Japanese Americans and blacks would have to be made as unalike as possible.

Double Dutch Double Cross 1973

Right before my parents moved my brother and me up and out to the suburbs—where I would lose my "black" voice and gain the "white" one that allows me as an adult to fool people like Lorenz—I remember falling in love with double Dutch. Even at nine years old, I knew that black girls in the city were good at twirling and jumping in and out of two ropes at the same time. But I was also painfully aware that I couldn't do it. My recollection is that I only learned to double Dutch properly on the day or so before we moved away. Whether this is a "true" memory or not I am uncertain, but I have this image of the older girls in my soon-to-be old neighborhood letting me jump and jump until I got it right. I guess it was their parting gift. And I remember, or at least I think I remember, feeling that being inside those crossing lines of ropes was the coolest thing I had ever done. The metaphors of double-crossing and double Dutch were made for that time in my life. A black family moving to the white suburbs and a little girl's belief that authentic black girlhood was defined by a skill that would be forever denied in the suburbs are the images that could easily work within the framework of the black/white color line. However, in this case, I first thought of the double Dutch metaphor during my research at the Chicago Historical Society. The relationship between blacks and Japanese Americans in Chicago over the past fifty years is another way to apply the notion of double Dutch to real life. Ironically, both my life and the history of Japanese Americans and blacks become more understandable with the imagery of staying in the space between two ropes that come together, cross, and then go out again in separate directions again and again—without ever touching.

According to the great relocation mythology that is constantly in the back of our minds today, Japanese Americans eventually overcame the stigma of Internment and the racism of postwar Chicago. Every group that came up from the stockyards and the foundries—or in the case of Japanese Americans, the Internment camps—took its turn at living the "Chicagoized" version of the American Dream. Except blacks. But these narratives did not come out of a vacuum. They figure prominently in the way researchers, individual citizens, and government officials think about race, employment, and housing today, in part because we learned to believe in the black/white color line by pointing to Japanese Americans as noncoloreds. And the fact that the great migration can be used as the primary narrative to describe race in Chicago, or in America for that matter, is a result of how well the great relocation of Japanese Americans to Chicago ironically supports the idea that the black migration was the primary migration. It isn't a major statement to say that racism in America has meant that different nonwhite groups have been used against each other, but it is not common to assert, as I am doing here, that race theory in America is rooted in the types of relationships that existed between Japanese Americans and blacks in Chicago right after World War II.

"Cablasian" pro golfer Tiger Woods aside, the black/white color line is an artificially created way of looking at race in America. It is sort of like Hoover Dam—man-made, but powerful nevertheless. The color line is at the root of Chicago's reign as race capital of America. It is also central to ideologies about who is deserving of, and what is, the American Dream/Experience. But we haven't ever really stopped to ponder that what we believe about the movement of raced labor to the city tells only one part of major political and economic shifts. Most Americans, scholars or not, have never heard of the three Japanese American students, but they have heard of and believe in the black/white color line. The double cross has meant Americans believing in the color line and denying the realities of Japanese American/black relations in Chicago—like those outlined in the three UCDS dissertations. Just as many other migrant groups' histories tell us, Japanese Americans followed word-of-mouth stories of the good life in Chicago. Yet once there, they realized that the life was not so good after all. My informants' lives reflect this. Even if they themselves did not move back and forth between Chicago and California, their relatives did. Japanese Americans have been left out of these kinds of investigations, but clearly they need to be studied as part of race history and not as special cases.

The idea that there was a color line between black and white was important, but we need to know how all the "others" were affected and in turn, how they affected the notion. In other words, what was the ideological product of such a system? Japanese Americans' great relocation to Chicago has figured in the double cross since its beginning, more than fifty years ago. But it is exactly because Chicago is and was at the center of what we think about race in America that the Japanese American great relocation and those who chronicled it challenge contemporary, canonical understandings of race and culture, yet go unmentioned because they do just that.

VOICE

Bill Murasaki

I was walking up Sheridan Road with two shopping bags that I had bought
at Jewel and then a young black boy, a teenager, comes up to me and asks,
"Where is the L station?" The L station?! You know, from Wilson you can
see that station. And I said, "It's right over there." And I didn't notice but
he came up to me with . . . he had a towel, a sweater or something, and he
ended up stealing seven or eight dollars from my side pocket. And another
time I was on the Howard L station platform waiting for the shuttle to go to
Skokie to visit my brother. And there were two colored boys, one in front of
me and one in back of me. I noticed a tugging here [points to pants pocket]
and I said, "Hey, what are you doing?" That time I lost twenty dollars.

Another time when I was living on Leland, I went out to buy the Sunday
paper and coming back I noticed a black boy in front of me and a black
boy across the street. You know, you don't think that there is going to be a
robbery. Then I walked up the steps to my place, and I opened the door
and they came and put a gun to my head. They said, "Take us to your
room." And I said, "I don't live here, fellas. I came here because I saw you
following me." But I wouldn't have taken them to my apartment. They
would have shot me. That time they took about sixty dollars from my back
pocket.

Another time when I was living at 920 Leland . . . I lived there for about
seventeen years. But I finally had to move out because I had been burglar-
ized about five times. I lived in a basement apartment. What finally made
me move was once a teenager that lived upstairs knocked at my door, yelling,
"Fire, fire! Get out right away!" I said, "OK." But I was suspicious. So I

Figure 7. Bill's bus stop at the intersection of Broadway and Sheridan, with the "bad" Jewel in the background.

started getting dressed and then he came back again five minutes later and pounds on the door. So instead of going up the stairway, I went outside and picked up a bottle. I walked around to the front and there were three teenagers on the second flight of stairs waiting for me. And I said, "Where is the fire?" And they just laughed, but I had my bottle in my hand and if they had come at me I'd have killed one of them. Of course I would have been killed. They would have killed me, I guess. Can you imagine? People living in the same apartment building would have killed me over the valuables that I would have brought out with me, if there had been a fire.

CHAPTER FOUR

"Can You Imagine?"

Race in Chicago through Japanese American Lenses

Since arriving in Chicago right after World War II, Japanese Americans have both affected and been affected by their positions within the raced realities of daily life in Chicago. As I emphasized in chapter 3, Japanese Americans' arrival in Chicago was reworked to fit existing (and evolving) notions of what it meant to be colored in urban America. In this chapter I continue to press this idea by concentrating on race in Chicago through the memories and observations of Nisei men and women, accounts directly told to me. Having lived in Chicago since the earliest waves of relocation during the 1940s and having arrived there as young men and women, these select voices represent a minority of minorities. They are not presented here in traditional oral history format; I have instead organized their personal narratives around life before and after Chicago in order to see how they came to see race in the way that they do today. Much of what is in this chapter was the result of our conversations about race in the United States, not from our first round of interviews, which usually began with my asking, "Can you tell me about your childhood and where you grew up?" I want to show you, in the way I was shown, how race looks in Chicago through a Japanese American lens.

What we see from that perspective are lives in which race and racial boundaries take on new meanings and dimensions. In this context what may seem to be simply the recollections of elderly Japanese Americans really are important accounts of how divisions among Americans have been constructed and reconstructed around the portmanteau of race.[1] These accounts alert us to two main points. First, Japanese American

lives reflect larger patterns of urbanization that have taken place throughout racialized postwar urban America. Second, these particular men and
women have developed an astute awareness of the ways that the idea of
race weaves in and out of their lives and those of their fellow Chicagoans.
This second point also emphasizes that these individuals look backward
from their positions as activists at the end of the twentieth century to
make sense of their racialized pasts and presents. Part of understanding
Japanese Americans' experience of race in Chicago is understanding the
ways that race in America affected Nisei long before they arrived in the
Midway metropolis. These men and women tell of lifelong experiences
as both racial and cultural outsiders, experiences that helped to create
the distaste for inequality and discrimination that fuels their activism
today. Their recollections are offered up as evidence that race through
Japanese American eyes is not necessarily centered around being as "non-
colored" as possible. For them, experiencing race in Chicago over the past
fifty years has left them with varied opinions about the connection between Japanese Americans and other nonwhites. But above all else their
stories tell us what life has been like for Japanese Americans since they
first began to relocate to Chicago. The realities of their lives have been
left out of accounts of race in Chicago, yet racial issues in postwar Chicago cannot be understood without paying close attention to race in
Japanese Americans' everyday lives. My research not only let me hear
about race in my informants' lives, but also to see their experiences
through my own ethnographic eye.

One day I was riding my bike up Broadway when I saw Bill Murasaki
waiting at a bus stop. I was just north of Irving Park Road, the boundary
between two very different neighborhoods. Although a marketing analysis firm has determined that both Wrigleyville/Lakeview and Uptown
are "a Bohemian Mix—a potpourri cluster characterized by youth, high
education and a potential to make a lot of money"—it seems that the
research people at Claritas Inc. had probably not actually crossed Irving
Park Road into Uptown.[2] While Wrigleyville/Lakeview does seem to fit
the description of a bohemian mix, Uptown is as ethnically diverse and
poor as Wrigleyville/Lakeview is white and gentrified. Uptown is the
home of the wig shops, rent-to-own appliance stores, drug treatment
centers, tattoo parlors, and corner taverns/liquor stores that are common
in just about every urban neighborhood where the working poor of
color live. But day by day, year by year, Uptown is losing these types of

businesses. It seems inevitable that one day the researchers' predictions will come true. The northward creep of upscale condominiums replacing demolished old buildings and businesses is taking place slowly but steadily up and down Sheridan Road and the surrounding streets. Yet even with all of the construction and transformation, Uptown is still no bohemian mix. At least it was not on the day that I saw Bill.

He was sitting at the bus stop in front of the Jewel-Osco grocery store and the Salvation Army resale shop. He wore a baseball cap, and his trademark shoulder-length silver hair was poking out from underneath. At three o'clock it was too early in the afternoon for the wealthy white men and women in suits to start arriving at the Gold's Gym that shared the building with the supermarket. I had discussed the food store with at least three different women on three different bus rides. Every time I was told without any prodding: "That store has rats"; "Girl, don't buy your greens there. Go down to the one where the white folks go"; or "They sure do make you pay that ghetto tax up in that Jewel." I had never seen any vermin in the store, but I had seen a noticeable difference between it and the one in Wrigleyville/Lakeview. The poor quality of food and the long lines of the Uptown store stood in stark contrast to what was available in a Jewel just a few miles south. The Salvation Army resale shop was next door to the Jewel complex. Right across the street was the once beautiful historical landmark, the Buena Memorial Presbyterian Church. The church was situated at a fork where the major streets of Sheridan Road and Broadway diverged or converged, depending on your direction. Later the following spring the church was torn down after years of being boarded up and used as a sanctuary of a different sort—for drugs, prostitution, and a place where street men and women could occasionally take refuge under its eaves. The sign in front of the long-abandoned church had said the same thing for the past three years: "Come unto me and find rest."

Bill was sandwiched between two black men in their thirties who were sitting on the bench's back. They didn't look as though they would do him any direct harm, but Bill seemed out of place and looked a little nervous. He was clutching a plastic shopping bag with the Jewel-Osco logo. Traffic was whizzing by, so I pushed my bike up over the curb and said hello. Bill didn't recognize me at first and seemed surprised. Bill told me that he had been out doing some shopping and was waiting to ride the bus up to Lawrence Avenue (the next major street) to get back home to Heiwa Terrace. Motioning to the sky and the dark gloomy clouds, Bill asked, "What are you doing on that bike on a day like today?" I countered, "I am coming from downtown. What are you doing out here at all, when it is so cold on a day like today?" We laughed and the two black men raised their eyebrows and checked us out. They seemed puzzled by our familiarity. An Asian woman passed by with a cart filled with both Jewel-Osco purchases and two young children. She kept her head down and pulled her coat a little tighter as she made her way down the block. It was cold and windy, and one of the first storms of the winter season was promising to arrive soon. Across the street a black man who appeared to be in his fifties and a white woman in her forties seemed to be looking for something on the sidewalk. They had large shopping bags full of pop cans. The man abruptly grabbed the woman's hand; they looked like they were having an argument. All of us at the bus stop watched them for a few seconds. I asked Bill if he wanted me to wait with him until the bus came. He told me that he would be OK and that I was smart to wear a helmet, seeing how crazy Chicago drivers were. I told him it was OK and waited with him for about ten minutes. He got on the bus slowly. The two men on the bench stayed where they were. The man and woman across the street had long since headed south toward Irving Park Road. I got back on my bike and continued northward up Sheridan Road, remembering all the times that Bill had told me about being robbed or threatened with robbery in the past thirty years as he waited for the bus or train or went shopping. I hoped that Bill would get to Heiwa Terrace safely. I thought about how over the course of fifty years Bill had seen the neighborhood go through the patterns of gradual decline—and now was seeing it go through a gradual process of gentrification.

What story does my encounter with Bill tell? Is it an example of how poor people of color and the elderly of every hue experience urban life in the United States at the turn of the century? Is it the story of one stubborn Nisei man who refuses to move to the suburbs and live with relatives while continuing to fight against racial discrimination—although his daily life tests his decisions? Does my perspective as a researcher of color color my observations? Of course the encounter allows for each of these interpretations.

The relocation of Japanese Americans to Chicago must be seen as part of the history of the racialized and age-based gentrification taking place on Chicago's North Side. This first section highlights race in the city as it is played out on the quotidian level for my informants. Their stories, memories, and current positions in the city are part of the larger story of what has happened in urban neighborhoods throughout the United States in the postwar era. The second section of the chapter links the experiences of life before arriving in Chicago, up to and including World War II, to those of life in Chicago.

No Further Problems

Unlike movements of cheap labor of color before and ever since, the relocation of Japanese Americans to Chicago's labor-hungry wartime economy was a controlled and regulated operation. In the words of Al Kawaii: "Chicago was a very popular place among the cities like Detroit, Philadelphia, and Cincinnati. It was convenient, especially from the two camps in Arkansas. You just took a train, the old 'IC' line right up here. But before you could leave a camp you had to have a job and so the companies would use recruiters to get you to sign up. As soon as you cleared security, they gave you twenty-five dollars plus whatever train fare you wanted and away you went."

Away you went for sure. It was convenient for Japanese Americans who wanted out of the boredom and psychological torture of Internment. So they came. Rose Yamamura remembers: "It was kind of a fun time for us. They had lots of activities and so it was kinda OK for everybody. And of course there were plenty of jobs. They weren't good jobs, but during and right after the war there were jobs. You may not have gotten the best professional job, but you could always get a job."

When Pearl Harbor was bombed in 1941, there were only 350 Japanese (mostly nationals) living in Chicago, and they were not concentrated in any one neighborhood. Most of them were Japanese government officials or restaurant workers. But during the war the numbers greatly increased, although of course this is not recorded in official decennial census data. By the end of the war it is estimated that there were close to 30,000 Japanese Americans living in the Chicago metropolitan area, mostly in clusters on the south and far north sides of the city. So the arrival of the relocatees in a few short years, while not a huge number when compared with Chicago's other minority groups, was part of the larger story of race as it played itself out in Chicago.[3]

In those early years the War Relocation Authority (WRA) office in Chicago was in charge of making sure that the newly arriving relocatees had places to stay and employment in the city. The WRA produced pamphlets and books to disseminate the right information about the relocatees. One of the few surviving publications from the Chicago WRA stated that, above all else, Chicagoans had to be convinced that Japanese Americans would not be a problem. Thus the *Speaker's Guide on Relocation in Chicago* advised speakers to emphasize that the "Japanese American situation in Chicago" would not bring "further problems" to the city (U.S. WRA 1945: 13). What were these further problems? The answer may lie in the guide's suggestion that speakers concentrate on the three areas Chicagoans might feel uneasy about—housing, racial discrimination, and neighborliness. The idea that racial discrimination was considered a separate category from either of the other two is a discussion in and of itself. However, leaving that conceptual point of interest aside for the moment, it is clear that the reference about no further trouble had to do with the other racial group migrating in large numbers to Chicago at the time—southern blacks. The federal government might not have been able to control blacks' movement to Chicago, but with Japanese Americans things would be different. They would be controlled and trouble-free.

From the very first waves of relocatees from every Internment camp in the country to Chicago in 1943, Japanese Americans were under close control and supervision by both the government and private business. On one hand, the WRA was eager to allow private business to take control of Japanese Americans' economic status. Yet on the other hand, for what were supposed to be security reasons, the WRA set down strict rules for the relocatees, rules that were designed to keep them as inconspicuous as possible. Bill Murasaki remembers: "See, the WRA that took care of us, they told us don't clump together, keep a low profile. They didn't encourage people to stick together... you know, establish a colony. You know, Chinese established Chinatown. But not the Japanese. They were told not to. And as a rule if there was any clustering, it wasn't too much. We never had a neighborhood of our own because the WRA wanted us to spread out. And they mentioned that when you [went] out in public to not go out in groups and to keep a low profile."

Perhaps the WRA knew what it was doing. Al Kawaii remembers going to the Aragon Ballroom, a famous Chicago nightspot, to listen to the trumpeter Harry James in the early years of resettlement: "He was there, so a lot of us went. There were a lot of Japanese at the Aragon that night. And so after that the management made a decision. There had been too many Japanese, so from then on there would be a quota of 5 percent. There were just too many of us for one place. I never went back."

While the WRA informally enforced what businesses like the Aragon Ballroom formally declared, the agency's policies on relocatee employment further linked Japanese Americans' new lives to their abilities to be cast as ideal urban citizens of color. In 1943, when Tom Watanabe left the Poston, Arizona, camp, he, like many internees, was eager to restart his life. As a young man with a pharmaceutical degree, he had hopes of making a life for himself. Yet looking back on what he calls his "release," Tom believes that "the basis of that release was whether or not you could hack it alone with some kind of education or talent. If you could be a good auto mechanic and they could use your skills, then you could go . . . if you would not be trouble for the government."

Al Kawaii takes this idea even further. He suggests that much of what went on with the relocation revolved around the cheap and readily available workforce Internment created for businesses prospering in Midwestern wartime economies:

> Someone should do some research on those employers who employed those people from camp. There were companies that were looking for employees. But they were looking for cheap labor. The defense industries were paying a whole lot more, of course, but for the most part, we could not get into defense industries. We could only work in places like Curtiss Candy, and printing presses like Cuneo Press and R. J. Donnelly. Cuneo used to print *Life* magazine. These were large companies that were not defense industries and they weren't paying much. But to us it meant an awful lot, because we were really being paid next to nothing in the concentration camp. There were probably some individuals and companies that really were concerned and wanted to help for Samaritan reasons. But I am sure there were others who said, "Hey! We don't care who they are as long as we can pay them cheap." It was just like migrant laborers.

Life and Resettlement on Leland (and All Points North and South)

Life has changed in Chicago's neighborhoods since the end of World War II. As the Claritas Inc. analysts suggest, today neighborhoods like Uptown, Lakeview, and Hyde Park are in flux. They are being upgraded, we are told, from the tenements of the working poor to the rehabbed two-flats of the urban pioneers who have the wealth and commitment

to revitalize "once grand neighborhoods." But these Chicago neighborhoods that are on the upswing today are the same places where Japanese
Americans settled in the years right after the war ended, despite WRA
attempts to prevent the creation of Midwestern Japantowns. Unlike the
stereotyped white urban professionals who make up the majority of the
newcomers to Bill's Uptown neighborhood, Japanese Americans moved
to blocks where they could afford to buy or rent (and were allowed to
buy or rent). Usually these neighborhoods were not the most desirable
in the city. During the early years of relocation and its successor term
"resettlement," Japanese Americans in Chicago were integral participants
in the patterns of gentrification that continue today throughout the city.[4]

Japanese Americans could not escape another urban pattern that was
well entrenched in Chicago's and its neighborhoods' race politics. Bill's
account of his older brother's experiences on the South Side and his attempts to escape "black boys" underscores the ways that race affected
the relocatees' lives and shaped their understandings of the world in
which they lived:

> My brother lived on the South Side when the neighborhood was
> practically all Swedish. Eventually the black people came in and my
> brother's car got broken into three times and then he saw Jane, my
> oldest niece, going to school. She was maybe five years old. She was
> being tugged by black boys, and then he thought he better get out before
> there was any danger of Jane getting hurt. So then he found a place on
> the North West Side of Chicago and was just about getting ready to take
> over the place when the owner said, "No, I can't sell it to you. I've got
> telephone calls saying that if you sell to a Jap, we are going to burn the
> house down."

This incident took place in 1957, and Bill's brother eventually bought a
house in the northern and mostly white and Jewish suburb of Skokie.
Although Bill did not make note of the irony in his brother's story, he
concluded by telling me that when blacks eventually began to move into
Skokie years later, they were harassed, whereas Japanese had not been.
He stated, "Jewish people shouldn't do that; they've had a lot of prejudice
against them, yet they were prejudiced against blacks, too. You know
that 'racism' is all over!"

One day when I went to visit Bill, I asked him to tell me as much as
he could about what Uptown had been like when he moved there in
1964. He had lived in other places around the city since the mid-1940s,

but had spent the longest part of his life in Chicago in Uptown. He began by describing what it was like when he was living on Leland and Sheridan, after years of living in Stanley Park in a hospital workers' dormitory. His new landlord was a Japanese American, and most of the tenants were Japanese Americans, too. It was an exciting time for Bill, living in Uptown. "It was a regular neighborhood back then. On Sheridan Road there were three very fancy places for women's shoes. Stores for women. Can you imagine? That is how stylish the place was." Right before he moved to Heiwa Terrace in 1981, Bill was the only Japanese American living in his Uptown apartment building. The longtime Nisei landlord had just sold the building and moved to Hawaii. It was then, Bill said, that the neighborhood had changed so much that he felt he could no longer safely live there. But Bill believes that Uptown is in decline, even as investors and urban professionals see healthy rehabilitation: "The whole place has deteriorated. I can't place an exact time when it started changing, but since I moved here the place has gone down. It happens slowly, so you don't even notice." Bill added, "Gradually, the people living on Leland, you know the Nisei, went back to California or Hawaii or wherever else they came from. And eventually the landlord had to rent to hillbillies. You know you have to rent to anyone."[5]

The slowness of change for those who live it every day is not hard to imagine. When I see photos from the turn of the century that show farm fields and open spaces and then compare them with those of the same areas fifty years later, I am struck by the slow change that even these photos seem to show. Although the photos from the fifties of smiling Nisei standing proudly on the steps of their new Uptown or Lakeview apartment buildings may seem different, fifty years is not that long, especially when I think about the lives that we all have lived on Chicago's North Side. Even though Bill remembers the Uptown that he moved into as being stylish and fashionable, there are others who, if alive, would think that the same period marked a downturn in the neighborhood. In 1952 John Drury suggested in the *Lincolnite*, a neighborhood publication, that the turn-of-the-century "group of wealthy Chicago businessmen who laid out country estates around a fashionable hotel of the period, the Lakeview House which stood at the intersection of Grace and Sheridan Road," might be astonished at how the neighborhood had changed.[6] Whether at the turn of the century, in the years following the end of World War II, or at the end of the twentieth century,

Figure 8. My Andersonville.

all our lives are connected in the ongoing slow process of constantly shifting races and classes—and in the ways we imagine what is going on around us. But for the Nisei who have lived through the changes over the past fifty years, even if the lines that divide neighborhoods and the people that live in them change slowly, race figures prominently in how they interpret their past. Al Kawaii, who has lived since 1950 in Rogers Park, a Far North Side neighborhood that shares a border with the suburb of Evanston, believes that there is a marked difference between the past and the present racialized Chicago:

> I think that way back in the 1950s there were much more distinctive lines of demarcation. This was a white neighborhood, this one Hispanic, this one was a black community. But I think over the years, gradually the lines have broken and we have no real lines. Oh, you still have them, but it's much less than it was back in the 1950s. I can remember even when we first came here in 1946, the black community was anything west of Cottage Grove and anything east was white. But over the years the lines of demarcation have changed and you have much more integration. Here in Rogers Park, we think that the Rogers Park/West Ridge area is probably one of the most diverse neighborhoods in the city and in the nation. For example, here you have a large African American population and right along Clark you have a lot of Mexicans, over on Devon by Western you have a lot of Indians and Pakistanis. Then here in West

Eglise de Dieu Haïtienne
Vendredi Priere   7 - 8:30 pm
Ecole du Dimanche   10 - 11 am
Dimanche Adoration 11:30 - 1:30 pm
           Evangélisation 6 - 8 pm
      Tel. 554-4895
HOI THANH TIN LANH VIET NAM NAZARENE

Figure 9. Tom's Uptown.

Rogers Park you have a large Jewish population. So it is really a diverse neighborhood. And for the most part you can tell which part is which, but still you get a lot of mixing.

The constantly shifting lines of which neighborhood is whose are not the only things that change and then change again. Tom Watanabe lived four blocks south of me; however, we technically lived in different neighborhoods. Tom lived in Uptown and I lived in Andersonville, yet we were just four blocks apart on Glenwood Avenue. We were separated by Foster Avenue, which ran east and west and, like so many other streets in Chicago, seemed to act as an electric fence to keep Chicagoans of different races separated. My side of Glenwood, north of Foster, at least until it reached Peterson, which served as another electric fence to keep a different set of groups apart, was a very different place from Tom's Glenwood, south of Foster. Tom's side of Glenwood was full of the same type of wonderful old buildings that were on the northern side, and there were plenty of well-kept lawns and houses with brand-new siding, too. Yet unlike Andersonville, Tom's part of Uptown was decidedly more "colored" and lower class than Andersonville. We lived in two different census tracts, to put it in more concrete terms. Houses where I lived had a median value of $500,000, while on Tom's side the value was $137,800.

During the first real push of gentrification in Uptown in the early 1990s, there was an effort by some Uptown newcomer rehabbers to change the name of Uptown completely. In 1993 one resident was quoted in the neighborhood paper, the *Monitor:* "This word Uptown should really be taken out of the language. . . . it has derogatory connotations." The article about Uptown included a photo of a "well-maintained house" that stood in "contrast to the run-down structures" in other sections. The white woman standing in front of the house with a high iron fence seemed to illustrate the changes that were taking place as the pockets of wealthy Far North Side residents began to increase.

I rode my bicycle past Tom's house whenever I headed downtown, and each time I was amazed at the mixture of people who lived in the small group of apartment buildings along the three-block area from Foster to the cemetery—Eastern Europeans, Southeast Asians, Mexicans, and Appalachian whites. During the summer, adults and children of every possible hue and nationality, it seemed, would sit outside the sturdy, but not well-kept, beige and brown brick buildings. Sometimes I stopped my bike to join the rest of the crowd. On one occasion they were watching what appeared to be a confrontation between two mothers— one Eastern European and the other a Latina—over a stolen bicycle. Indeed, the interactions among the children always seemed to echo what was probably going on inside the buildings. These were the outward signs of too little money, too many people, and too many different languages in tiny apartments.

One day when I stopped by Tom's house he served me cake and tea and we talked about the changes that had been taking place on this side of Glenwood since he and his own family had arrived there in 1955:

> When we got here they told us it was a Scandinavian community. But we bought this house from a Chinese family. It was a mixed community even then. I suppose that there was a time that if you didn't come over on the Mayflower you wouldn't have been allowed to live here. I guess most of the Scandinavians couldn't really tell the difference between Chinese and Japanese and so nobody ever really said anything to us. Well, I suppose "never" is too strong a word. And I think about ten or fifteen years ago, not too long after the Vietnam War, when our government decided out of a guilty conscience to take care of these displaced people, this neighborhood started to really change. Chicago took a whole lot of the Southeast Asians and they came here. I suppose around 1965, I started to see more African Americans and Hispanics.

I asked Tom about the strangeness of the neighborhood boundaries. I wondered if it had always been like this, with the strict boundaries in both name and reality. He answered: "I don't know where Andersonville stops or starts. Sometimes it's called Uptown but then they tell me that further along it becomes Rogers Park and a little bit west it is called Ravenswood. They might say that the neighborhood is getting better these days, but I have been to meetings where they talk about gays and lesbians getting beat up around here. How can it be getting better when you have that going on?" For Tom the neighborhood was always changing, and although some might see it as getting better, he knew that it depended on whom you asked.

Rose Yamamura lives in the Lakeview area, the neighborhood that has the "good" Jewel supermarket. She too sees race, class, and sexuality as the main identifiers of who has come and gone and come again to the neighborhood that she has lived in since 1955. The question of whether or not Lakeview is a "Yuppieville" is an interesting one for Rose:

> Oh yes. It is not only Yuppieville, but it is the gay area. It is very interesting how it evolved. When we first came here it was a Swedish neighborhood. My parents and I bought this house from an Italian-Irish family, and our next door neighbors were Swedish. This was the time when all the Swedes were starting to move out of the neighborhood. And then a lot of Japanese families bought buildings around here. I would say there must have been, oh god, maybe a dozen just on this street alone. And then in the late sixties or so we started to get in some people who were kind of undesirable. I'll just put it that way. They were Puerto Ricans and they had many, many children. And a lot of Japanese got discouraged about that and so they sold and moved out. But some of us remained—about seven or eight houses. Today there are only four houses [of Japanese Americans] left.

Rose believes that in the 1950s and 1960s there were only about fifty Japanese American families in the Lakeview area. The area stretches from Belmont and Addison on the north and south and from Clark to Broadway on the east and west. Today the area is known as Chicago's "Boystown." It is the site for the annual Gay Pride Parade, as well as being the neighborhood that borders Wrigley Field, the major league baseball stadium. The mixture in the neighborhood is amazing, especially on select summer days. It seemed as though whenever the sun came out in Lakeview, every resident and visitor came out, too. It was noticeable, although Rose had a black tenant, that there were few people of

Figure 10. Asian Village Shopping Center, Uptown.

color who lived in Lakeview, even if they worked there during the day. Rose told me: "I was always very conscious that Chicago was a very segregated city. You knew that whites lived here and blacks lived there and we were always conscious of that from the beginning. But it wasn't fear."

One day when I was visiting Rose, we walked down the stairs from her second-floor apartment and commented on the varieties of people making their way up and down the street. Even though Rose lived on a small residential street, it was a busy thoroughfare. Patrons from the many bookstores, restaurants, garden shops, cafés, and "alternative" clothing boutiques shared the sidewalk with well-heeled Chicago Cubs fans en route to the big game. But this present still had remnants of the past wave of urban pioneerism. Just off Rose's street on the major street of Clark, Lakeview's past met its present. Bars with names like "The Manhole" and shops festooned with gay pride rainbow paraphernalia stand next door to places like the Star Market and the Nisei Lounge. Both are remnants from the time in the mid-1950s when Lakeview was the closest thing Chicago had to a Japantown.

Rose believes that the transformation from a neighborhood in decline, one of the few places where she and her parents could afford to buy a house in the 1950s, to the highly-sought-after trendy place that she lives in today was due to two successive waves of gay homeowners:

For some reason I remember when it all first started. I went to buy a Christmas tree on Broadway. This would have been in the early 1980s. And I remember, it was before all of this rehabbing happened. I asked the man if he would deliver the tree for me. He asked me where I lived and I told him. And he said, "Oh, that is the up-and-coming street." I said, "Oh really. That's nice." And then, it did. It started to come up. There were a number of gays who originally came here around then. They came, they bought, and renovated. But I have been noticing over the last five or six years that they've started to buy again. And you know they do a very good job of keeping up their property. I really like that. They are good neighbors.

Rose does not see this gentrification process as all good, however: "Rents are out of sight here. I do see kids playing around, but how can an average family afford living here?"

There is a mixture of feelings among these Nisei about the processes of gentrification. Yet no matter what their opinions, they all seem to agree on what it was like for them to arrive in a city in which they were not considered to be like whites. Perhaps Bill Murasaki's memory of first arriving in Chicago says it best:

Sure I have felt discrimination. When I first arrived in Chicago, I was looking for an apartment. The first place that I went was on Winthrop. At that time Winthrop was a regular white neighborhood, not like now. Now it is mostly all black or Vietnamese. A man leaned out from the second floor and called out to me, "We don't rent to Orientals." If he had spoken to me face to face, I would have *smacked* him. I don't care if I had been killed. It was just a matter of . . . if after you have been in a concentration camp and then come out to face that. I was so mad. And you know he spoke with broken English. You know, he was a foreigner. I don't know what kind of European [that man was], but my brother lives in Skokie with Polish neighbors and you couldn't find better people. But of course when Heiwa Terrace was built, the elderly Issei didn't come in. They thought that it was welfare. Charity. They should have come in. This neighborhood isn't so bad. Of course, some of them did not like the neighborhood.

Other Awareness

My informants' life histories show their awareness of the color-line ideology in Chicago. They rarely had a choice to ignore their positions within the everyday goings-on of race. From the beginning they looked at race in Chicago with a sophisticated awareness of the impact of the black/white color line on their daily lives. They understood that their lives, and the lives of other Japanese Americans in the city, were affected by what happened to other people of color—especially when it came to employment opportunities. This other awareness is not just about what happened when they got to Chicago, but also about their childhood experiences with race. Their lives before they arrived in Chicago trained them to see their world through lenses that paid close attention to their position within racial hierarchies and the inequity embedded in such rankings. But beyond that, their life histories, and their work histories in particular, point to possible reasons for their attention to details that many others either did not or could not dare to acknowledge.

The country's reaction to Japanese Americans during World War II meant that Japanese Americans were relocated to places where very few Asian Americans had lived or visited before the war. Internment camps, assembly centers, military installations, universities, and factory jobs all became the places where Japanese Americans were most likely to be found during the war. These places, as mandated by Executive Order 9066, were far away from the West Coast, where the great majority of Japanese Americans had lived prior to World War II. Japanese Americans became a part of daily life in southern towns, isolated western ranches, and northern urban neighborhoods. Beyond the discrimination that was inherent in their forced removal from the West Coast, Internment and relocation brought a new awareness of race to Japanese Americans. They arrived in places with established patterns of dealing with people of color. There were eating establishments, theaters, and buses that had never served Japanese American patrons, not to mention the segregated military. Even if Japanese Americans were neither black nor Native American, they were not white, either. It was a time when being Japanese was not just a race issue, but for many Americans an issue of loyalty to the country. In such circumstances, it would have been impossible for most if not all Japanese Americans to ignore the impact on their own lives as nonwhites. Race as seen through Japanese American eyes not only tells us the story of Japanese Americans, but also of the development of a sophisticated awareness of the impact of the black/white color line on their lives and what that awareness has allowed them to "see" from their positions within Chicago's postwar racial hierarchies.

Al was seventy-one years old when I first met him in 1995. Throughout my time working with the Human Rights Committee, I probably developed the closest relationship with Al. It may have been because we seemed to look at the world through the same type of lens, despite our differences in gender, race, and age. The first time he invited me to his house in the fall of 1995, I began our interview by reminding him that I was trying to find out about the relationship between blacks and Japanese in Chicago. Al told me that the day before he had been playing golf with two of his "black" friends. He spoke in a way that signaled a mutual understanding about the way some whites would eagerly tell us about their minority "friends." I asked back in the same tone, "You've got black friends?" We both laughed. From this first interview onward, I believed that Al should have been an anthropologist. His observations and life-long commitment to thinking about the world around him make him one of the most important influences on my belief that the relationships between Japanese Americans and blacks are so similar and intertwined that they have been major factors in the articulation of race in the United States.

Al was born in 1924 in Los Angeles, the fifth of six children. His father was an older man who had returned to Japan to marry a younger woman and bring her back to California. His parents, both from Wakayama prefecture, Japan, were typical of the Issei generation. His father, like many other Issei, had been a farmer in Japan, a businessman in Little Tokyo until the Great Depression forced him out of business, and, until World War II, what Al called a fertilizer salesperson. Al's family went through tough times, and his mother became what he called an "evangelist." The tone in Al's voice when he told me this indicated that he had doubts about his mother's religious choices and their implications for his family. Al and his brothers and sisters were "brainwashed" into the Seventh Day Adventist church, as his mother "was into Christianity and that was her life." When he was four or five years old, the family moved to Keystone, California (now called Carson City), where his family lived until the war broke out. Al was seventeen at the time.

The other reason I feel a close bond with Al is that I identified with his own appraisal of his view of the world. He often said that his child-hood had made him extremely aware of being different, even among those who were considered different, which in turn had made him notice throughout his life how the differences among people are played out. He told me: "It was difficult being Japanese in California and then on top of that, while most of our Japanese friends were either Buddhists or nonreligious, we were Seventh Day Adventists. We were not really in step with most of the people. We just didn't fit in too well." Although the prevailing view of Japanese American communities before Internment is one of tightly knit groups of people with shared cultural values, Al's feeling that he and his family were not like everybody else stands in stark contradiction to prevalent views of early Japanese American communities as monolithic.

Al's account of feeling different from other "others" would fit nicely into the theories about otherness, identity, and difference that are widely debated throughout the social sciences and humanities. It draws our attention to and offers an explanation for why he and other Japanese Americans who have this awareness see the world as they do. As outsiders among outsiders, Al and the rest of the committee members developed a way of viewing their positions and the lives of others with an eye for the details that many people are not aware of or don't care to notice. Thus some of Al's most vivid memories from his childhood and his years as a soldier during World War II in the 442nd Division in Europe center around this kind of awareness. Al and others in the Human Rights Committee developed such an awareness both because of and in spite of their positions as Japanese Americans.

Al still remembers when his white eighth-grade teacher, Mrs. Borders, tried to talk him out of going to college prep courses when he entered high school, despite the fact that he was probably one of the top three or four students in his graduating class. "At the time she was thinking that even with a college degree but never getting any jobs, maybe I was better off doing something where I might get a job. I still remember that. It is peculiar how you remember certain things in life and you forget the vast majority of what has happened." For Al, an awareness of the hierarchy of races began sometime around high school:

> Even though for the most part Japanese faced all sorts of discrimination, they were still able to lease these farmlands. They would employ Mexicans as labor—stoop labor. And among Japanese Americans there was definitely a feeling of superiority over Mexicans. They looked down on the Mexicans because for the most part they were the laborers. And there was a carryover to today. Japanese Americans are just as racist as any group when they look at blacks or Mexicans. Like if you look at the Prop. 187, I am guessing a good 60 percent or more of my friends and colleagues probably voted for it.

Still, Al says:

> At our high school I would guesstimate that at least 15 percent were
> Mexican and we had many Mexican friends. But from the time you
> entered elementary school to high school, you knew that there were
> certain lines. For example, there were a lot of pretty Mexican girls. But
> you knew that you didn't date Mexican girls or white girls. You were
> supposed to date your own. So everybody understood that. Even though
> in school in clubs, classes, and teams there was a nice mix of kids, you
> went home to your own community. There was a line of demarcation.
> No one ever said anything. It was just understood. We enjoyed our high
> school years, but we more or less knew our place.

But when Al recently attended his fiftieth high school class reunion,
he tried to engage his white classmates, many of whom he still considers
to be good friends, in talking about those early years:

> I kept thinking to myself, if only I could get them to talk about how
> they felt during those early years. How did they feel about us after Pearl
> Harbor? But it was so hard when you tried to ask them. You knew they
> were not going to come out and say, "At one time I thought those
> damned Japs . . ." I was kind of disappointed that I couldn't get around
> that and get to what they really had felt.

For Tom Watanabe, awareness about racial differences among people
and how these perceived differences affected the lives of everyone began
during his high school years as well. Tom was born five years earlier
than Al and grew up further south, along the California-Mexico border.
But life in Brawley, California, created the same types of memories for
Tom that life near Los Angeles did for Al. Tom's family—mother, father,
and four siblings—were farmers, as were most of the eight hundred
Japanese American families in the area during the 1920s and 1930s, farming small crops like cantaloupe, melons, lettuce, tomatoes, and cucum-
bers. Tom remembers his neighbors as a diverse group of people, most
of whom were involved in agriculture in some way:

> The biggest number ethnically would have been people from Mexico
> and then Caucasians. Then came the Asians. The biggest number would
> have been Japanese and a very few Chinese and Filipinos. There were
> also small bits of people from India. You know, they wore turbans and
> stuff. Mostly everybody was farmers, but the Indians and Filipinos were
> the laborers. African Americans were just a small group, and they too
> farmed a bit. We mostly ran into them in high school. But mostly as kids
> we mingled with Mexicans and Caucasians.

Tom believes that the lines that were drawn among Brawley's youth by virtue of their racial and economic differences were not as strict in high school as they were outside of school. He remembers:

> I think that the intermingling came at the high school level. The schools were segregated back then, and if you were not Japanese or Caucasian... you were separated at the grammar school level. But at the high school level everybody who went to school, or at least who was able to continue school, went to the same high school. Japanese kids did not drop out and African Americans, if they started, most of them finished, too. The ones that were dropping out were the Mexicans. Not because they didn't like school. It was mostly because they were migrants and they had to follow the work and their families. There wasn't much tension, though. Sometimes remarks were made, you know, racial slurs. But I never encountered a "let's go and get those guys" situation.

Brawley was indeed a multiracial community, long before the term became popular. As in every town, city, and outpost where race, work, and gender intersect, Brawley taught Tom a few lessons about sexual politics. Just as Al knew better than to ask Mexican girls out on dates because of unspoken laws, so Tom saw and heard about relationships between Asian men and white women. One day during one of our interviews, we were talking about Karen Isaksen Leonard's book about Brawley, *Making Ethnic Choices* (1992). Hesitating for a moment, Tom warned me that he was about to tell me "something bad":

> The Indians were not allowed to bring womenfolk with them and so they would all live together in one place. And neither could the Filipinos. And so both the Indians and the Filipinos would get a Caucasian woman and share her among themselves. I don't know how much or even how they could afford to pay these women, but they could always find a white woman. They were something like a live-in prostitute. When we would see them in a nice car driving down the road with one gal and eight guys in the car, we all would say, "Ooo! Look at that!"

Both Tom and Al were enlisted men during World War II. But the war's impact on Al is of particular note. As a young soldier traveling around the United States and then in Europe, Al learned that racial discrimination and prejudice were not so simple as white versus black. Al was one of the first to volunteer from a relocation camp in Jerome, Arkansas, where he had been living for six months with his mother and two sisters. His father had been taken away by federal agents in the first few days after the bombing of Pearl Harbor and was detained in New

Mexico. His other siblings were scattered throughout the country—a sister who was married to a Mexican American and living with him, a brother who was in college, and another brother who was in the army. Despite the rumors that were circulating throughout the Jerome camp that it was foolish to volunteer, Al and his four friends decided to go ahead. They shaved their heads, which Al remembers in retrospect as one of the strangest things they could have done as young Nisei men. They decided that they would get jobs in Chicago, menial of course, while waiting to be called to duty. As the days went by, each of the friends was called one by one. Al was left alone. He decided to travel by bus to see his father, who was imprisoned, like many other Issei men who had been community leaders before the war, in the federal detention center in Santa Fe, New Mexico. For Al, who was barely eighteen years old, it was both thrilling and saddening. The trip is one of his earliest, but by no means only, memories of experiencing face-to-face discrimination:

> I remember one stop. I can't remember whether it was Montana or Wyoming, but we stopped for a lunch break or something. I was going to have something to eat, and the guy behind the counter said, "Sorry, we don't serve your kind here." So I didn't have my lunch. That's the first time I think that I experienced that kind of racism. And then I think the second time was right here in Chicago. I believe I was in uniform and I went to a bar. And the bartender said, "We don't serve your kind here." But he thought that I was an Indian, because he then repeated, "We don't serve drinks to Indians."

Nisei soldiers like Al served their country in a segregated unit with white officers. There were only 3,600 mainland-born Nisei soldiers who volunteered to serve in the segregated 442nd Regimental Combat Team. The great majority of Nisei soldiers who fought in World War II were Hawaiian natives.[7] In fact, Al was one of a handful of volunteers from the Jerome camp. He believes that there were only about twenty young men who enlisted after military officials visited in the hopes of encouraging Nisei volunteers. Al feels that he volunteered for the same reason that many others did: he thought that his enlisting might help get his father out of New Mexico so that he could rejoin the rest of the family in Arkansas.

Al had to go through boot camp at Camp Shelby, Mississippi. The arrival of thousands of Japanese American soldiers at the field training site near Hattiesburg was probably like nothing the area had ever experienced. The public transportation needs of the military—which meant trains and buses crowded with servicemen—quickly intersected with old rules about race and segregation. Traveling to and around Camp Shelby, Mississippi, Al remembers being forced to choose (or have chosen for him) his place in southern hierarchies:

> I was on a train near Camp Shelby. Man, was it crowded. But then I saw that there were some seats. So I went down and sat. And a guy said, "Hey, you can't sit there. That's for colored folks!" And I said, "I have got a seat and I am staying here." But in terms of the washrooms, I think we were instructed at Camp Shelby to use the white washrooms. I remember that there were soldiers who were Hawaiian Islanders and some of them were really dark. When we were in Hattiesburg, sometimes a bus driver might say something to them about going to the back of the bus and they would start fights and so forth. It was a problem when you took public transportation. But at the time you didn't give it much thought. We knew that there were unwritten laws and that was the way things were.[8]

Tom also experienced similar conflicts when he was in basic training in Texas. Tom was part of the Counter Intelligence Corps, the other arm of the military in which Japanese Americans were allowed to serve during the war. In Texas, too, being Japanese American meant being read by the existing racial distinctions. This translated into Tom's being called John Chinaman everywhere he went, but on buses he was told that he could not ride in the back of the bus because "that was for black people."

Even after Al Kawaii left boot camp to fight in the "Champagne Campaign" in the south of France, he continued to see the effect of unwritten laws about race on Japanese American soldiers. Al arrived in Europe just as the 442nd was pulling back from the Battle of the Lost Battalion at the Arno River. Al describes this as one of the saddest nights he ever spent, as he went around asking about his friends in pouring rain and learning that two of his four buddies had been killed in the battle. During the Allied Occupation, Al and many of the Nisei soldiers were stationed in Milan with the 92nd, a black unit nicknamed the "9 Deuce" or Buffalo Division. When we talked about those days after the war had ended, Al told me with a laugh that while other soldiers were out "looking for what men look for," he went to the opera and museums. He attributed that to still being under the influence of his Seventh Day Adventist background. But even though Al may not have actively been a part of the sexual politics of soldiers looking for love, he was able to see how the quest for white European women divided soldiers along racial lines:

> I can still remember, let's say what you would call fights between blacks and whites over women. 'Cause you know the black troops, they had candy and cigarettes just like the white troops ... and there were women that ... But I remember some of our guys [Japanese Americans] talking about these black folks. And from what they said they were just as biased as the white guys. There was one guy in particular who was half Mexican and half Japanese and he would get real uptight about these black soldiers with white women. You would hear people saying, "Those niggers ..." Coming from the background that we have in these United States, it wasn't strange at all for Nisei to be saying those kinds of things.

Japanese American soldiers were in a strange place indeed. Not only because their families were interned while they fought for democracy, but also because their lives in the military were intertwined with blacks. Whether like Al, who remembers his years as a soldier of color in World War II with irony, or like the half Japanese American, half Mexican soldier who wanted to protect European white womanhood from menacing black troops, Japanese American soldiers were aware of, and made decisions about, how to deal with their own fluctuating positions along the color line.

Al's life continued after he got out of the military. As he puts it, "We all had to make some decisions about what to do with our lives after the war and mine was to go to school and become a teacher. My good buddy decided to go to work and I went to Roosevelt University here in Chicago." Al not only became a teacher but also went on to get married and become the first Asian American principal in the Chicago Public School system. Al's interpretation of why and how he achieved the status of principal is another telling example of the level of complex racial awareness Japanese Americans were forced to develop in their daily lives.

Al began teaching in 1953 as a substitute seventh-grade teacher in an all-white school with an all-white faculty on the North Side. The principal liked what he saw and asked Al to stay on; he did, until 1961. Al looks back on all of his teaching positions with fondness, but remembers that he was concerned about how the kids would respond to him: "They had never had a nonwhite teacher before, and before the war, in California, you could not get a job teaching." In 1961 Al became an assistant principal on the South Side at an all-black school. He stayed there until 1964, when he received his promotion to principal. He describes the elementary school he was assigned to in Hyde Park on the South Side:

> When I was first assigned as principal I thought about it a lot. I was lucky because Hyde Park is a rich professional/upper-middle-class neighborhood with blacks, whites, and others. And in 1964 the school that I was principal at was probably the best-integrated school in Chicago—a desegregated school. We had a good mix of blacks, whites, and a few Asians.

In just three years, Al was moved again. In 1967 he was appointed to a slightly larger and older school also on the South Side. But just as Al was changing jobs, Chicago was changing, too. Al recalls:

> In less than three years the neighborhood went from being almost 100 percent white to almost 100 percent black. So this new school they gave me was going through some serious changes. When I got there it was probably about 90 percent black and 10 percent white and others. The students came from all different kinds of classes. And at that time there was an influx of gangs. The Blackstone Rangers, which were the forerunners of the El Rukns, and their rival gangs would come over from the West Side. One of the things I remember about being there was that around 1968 when [Martin Luther] King was assassinated, there was a lot of rioting going on. We didn't have any riots on the South Side, but you knew you had to be careful. And I remember walking around the outside of the school, making sure everything was all right, and as I was doing this a black fellow across the street yelled at me, "It's a good thing you ain't white!"... People talk about whether Japanese Americans are closer to black or white [laughter]. You have to see that with a white person he may have gotten upset, but he didn't identify me as being white.

According to Al, 1968 through 1969 were "turbulent times in Chicago and those King riots were just the beginning." So in 1969 Al was moved yet again. This time he was given a tremendous promotion to a high school that had just been the site for one of the largest and most tension-filled student riots in the nation. The student population at the time was about 50 percent black, 40 percent Latino, and 10 percent white. The riots escalated over a series of days as students made many demands, including the removal of the white principal and the firing of many white teachers. Al puts his promotion into the context of what was going on in the city of Chicago at the time:

You have to understand that in those days there was a definite system in terms of promotions. In order to become a principal at a high school you would have to serve as an elementary school principal for at least fifteen to twenty years, and if you were lucky you got a high school appointment. I was promoted to be a high school principal in just five years. But I have to tell you, I earned every penny of my salary there.

He earned every penny of his salary because the school board must have thought

not being white, not being black, not being Hispanic, that I would go in being sort of a neutral factor. And to some degree I think that it may have worked the way they wanted, but at the same time I had to come to the job as an individual. There were different factions of students and teachers, some of whom were very militant. At Tyler there were gangs like the Latin Kings and the Morgan Deuces which would often get into conflicts with white gangs. Sporting events were bad for rivalries, too. And through all of this the white teachers were very defensive, and the teachers union was getting involved. It was a difficult time. But I like to think that I did a good job.

The school board was not finished shaping Al's career. In the fall of 1975, on the way back from taking his daughter to college in southern Illinois, Al heard a news story on the car radio that he believes signaled yet another transfer for him:

This was the time of the desegregation of the administrators in the Chicago Public Schools. And there were calls to see black principals in the white schools. And I was listening to this thinking, here we go again. There were two all-white high schools at the time, and I thought to myself, I bet they send me to one of those two instead of sending a black principal. And lo and behold in September that's exactly what happened. I was sent to Kennedy High School near O'Hare Airport.

But it was also a time of desegregation and busing for students. After many years as a teacher and an administrator at a variety of Chicago public schools, Al may very well have been the most capable principal for a school like Kennedy. However, once he got there, he was troubled by what was taking place in the name of desegregation:

About two years after I was there, we started out with a small group of maybe sixty black students from the West Side. It was touch and go for about a year and a half, because out there near the airport we have serious bigotry. On top of the community's prejudice, these were not exactly the best students who were coming from the West Side. I've often thought that if we had the black students who lived in Hyde Park or Kenwood—good students who would have been able to do well in school—that it would have been a much easier transition.

Al retired from the Chicago Public School system in 1989. He had been principal at Kennedy for thirteen years. He believes that today the school is a well-integrated high school with a well-mixed population of black, white, and Asian students—and still probably one of the best high schools in the city. Al is well-known throughout the city, and on two occasions I have seen former students greet him. These are people who are now in their twenties and thirties but still come up to him with nervous smiles. I can imagine him walking up and down the halls of Kennedy and all the other schools where he worked and kids remembering him, not because he was Japanese American but because of how he treated them.

In the end, the reality that the Chicago School Board consistently called upon Al to defuse racially volatile situations cannot be ignored. Al says:

I feel that in a sense the school system has used me. They put me in certain spots where they felt that me not being white, not being black, not being Hispanic might have worked to their advantage. I have to say, too, that it worked to my advantage. The positions that I had through the years would have taken a very long time to achieve in ordinary circumstances. I was fortunate to be at the right place at the right time, although those were very difficult years for me. When I think about them now I think, "How did I survive all that?" But they were great experiences.

For Rose Yamamura it may have been her trip to Japan when she was sixteen years old that marked the beginning of an "other awareness." Rose was an only child born to a fairly successful Issei couple who operated a hotel and hop yards in Portland, Oregon. Although Rose's family's business was in the city, Rose grew up in the outskirts of Portland. Rose's father had come to the United States and was a prominent businessman and community leader, a distinction that would work against him once the war with Japan began in 1941. A man of many talents, he graduated from law school, owned interest in a lumber mill in Canada, and after his time in a federal detention center in New Mexico, opened up a real estate office in Chicago. Rose's mother was a housewife, but had been "raised as a tomboy" in Hiroshima prefecture and was the daughter of a respected physician. Rose herself grew up in a town that was powered by logging, shipping, and cheese. She laughingly describes her childhood home today as "still a cheese town." Like Al and Tom, Rose began to pay close attention to race-created hierarchies when she entered high school:

> Where I went to school there was only one other Japanese in the whole class. There were only five hundred people in the whole town and there were probably only two or three African Americans. I think there were five nonwhites and the rest were white. So I think that those of us who attended schools like that were very conscious of the fact that we were not white. And I think that the telling thing was that as soon as we got into high school and people started becoming social, you know dances and things, we were excluded. So you were very conscious of things, events, where you did not belong.

When Rose was a teenager her mother decided to finally take the trip back to Japan that her husband had promised her. Rose went with her mother and met her maternal relatives for the first time. She was shocked by the "male chauvinism" she saw in Japan. During that trip the realities of inequality that divided people—race, class, gender, nation—influenced the way that Rose saw her place in the world:

> Japan was already at war with China, and you know that we were subjected to the same kind of propaganda that every other American was then. Japan was short on leather and food and all sorts of things, so when I would ride the bus everyone would stare at my leather shoes and glare. My mother and I were really uncomfortable. But the other thing that really bothered me about Japan, and I have always remembered this, was the way that my mother's family treated their maid. She was treated in a way that I could never cope with. She was not allowed to use the same dishes as the family. She was never allowed to come into the living room except to clean. When I walked down to the village with her one day, I was told to make her walk behind me. I was really upset about that. So when my mother and I left to come back to the States, I gave her this nice little angora sweater. It sounds so bad to say that, but that was what I did in protest.

After she returned from Japan, Rose's life changed drastically. Her father was picked up and taken away to New Mexico in one of the first

FBI sweeps after the bombing in Pearl Harbor in December 1941. Rose and her mother did the best they could to manage the hotel until May of the next year. Then like so many other Japanese Americans, both Rose and her mother packed up their belongings and went to the Minidoka Internment camp. Rose was a senior in high school. It was not until April 1943 that Rose left the camp, to attend college at Denver University. Because she had little money, Rose eventually got a position helping a white family with their small child in exchange for room and board. She remembers that the people she worked for in Colorado "were not rich, but the child was a brat. In actuality they were nice and even encouraged me to transfer to University of Wisconsin because at that time I wanted to major in journalism. But when I first went there they asked me if I minded eating in the kitchen alone. I told them that I didn't mind." This was a strange twist of fate for Rose, who could not help but remember her maternal family's maid back in Japan as she worked as a domestic in Denver.

Rose eventually did transfer to the University of Wisconsin, where she was one of the few female math majors in the university. She remembers that "the professors would make me sit in the front of the classroom and the male students would make fun of me. I was the only woman in many of my classes." In another instance, a well-intentioned white friend's attempts to invite Rose home for Christmas were thwarted because the girl's foster family told her that Rose was not welcome in their rural town. A trip to the dentist in Milwaukee provided Rose with what she calls "a very interesting experience":

> Somebody told me that I should go see Doctor Sweeney. I will always remember that name. And so I went to him, and he looked at me. I mean *looked* at me. He wanted to know what I was. I said, "I am Japanese." He said, "But your skin is so white." Can you believe it? Looking back, I don't think that he meant to be discriminatory. I think he had seen these pictures and assumed that I was going to be dark with buckteeth and thick Coke-bottle glasses. I was so intimidated that I just walked out and was afraid to go back.

After graduating Rose eventually moved to Chicago to be with her parents. Her father and mother had lost everything during the Internment, and Rose describes those years as hard ones for her family, even while they were good ones for the relocatees in general. Her father was diagnosed with cancer in the mid-1950s and died a few years later, after the family moved to the house that Rose lives in today. Rose speaks of these years with a sense of humor, but a humor that comes out in bitter tones sometimes. It was not with sadness that she told these stories to me, but with an anger that was still strong after fifty years.

Today Rose is semiretired. On the day that she invited me over to talk about her employment history, she could only speak to me for an hour and a half because she had to get the flowers for the flower arranging class she teaches out of her home. But Rose has no apologies to make for never having what she calls a professional career. Rose has had many jobs throughout her life. She worked as a bookkeeper, a lead payroll clerk, an administrative assistant at a private art club, and finally as a business manager for a wealthy surgeon, a job she got when she was fifty years old. Despite having a math degree from one of the top universities in the country, Rose feels that her employment history is a mixture of discrimination and, surprisingly, luck: "I've been very lucky. I am going to tell you this. I have been very, very fortunate. I have really come out ahead. I mean I have never had what you would call a real professional job, but I've always had good jobs and come out really well. That couldn't happen today."

Bill, like Rose, spent most of his life in a string of jobs. He and Rose are the truth behind the fiction that Nisei arrived in Chicago, got married, moved to the suburbs, and raised fully assimilated Sansei children. Bill never married, has lived on the North Side of the city for most of his life, and has had a string of unskilled labor jobs in which he worked hard but never moved beyond the entry level. Bill's employment history, besides showing us our misleading notions of Japanese American economic success, also demonstrates Japanese Americans' awareness of their positions in highly racialized workplaces.

Bill has had three long-term jobs. Two of them have been in hospitals in the Chicago area. But even the third long-term job, working in the stock room of a national drugstore chain with headquarters in Chicago, lasted only a few years. When Bill talks about his work history, he speaks with excitement and vivid detail about his years at Stanley Park Hospital from 1946 to 1953, where he enjoyed working as an orderly/technician at the suburban hospital. But during these years, Bill says he began to think about how his position, and the positions of other unskilled and semiskilled workers, were affected by the race and class hierarchies in the hospital.

After arriving in Chicago at the end of the war from an Internment camp in Colorado, Bill immediately looked for work anywhere he could find it. By 1946 he had found his job at Stanley Park Hospital.[9] He was hired as a transporter of patients, but when he expressed an interest in wanting to take X rays, a skill he taught himself in camp from manuals when the technician was sent away and never returned, he eventually became a technician-orderly. He is proud that they had to invent this special job title just for him. Bill still had to transport patients, but the radiology department had him take all the dental X rays. He recounts:

> At first I was a flunky. Taking people back and forth. You know, a gofer.
> Later on I asked the head technician if I could take films. She said that
> when we have a charity patient you can try one. The radiologist was
> surprised and asked who was the wizard that took those pictures. The
> head radiologist wanted to send me to the university to take a class on
> how to take films, but then a dentist that would come to the hospital saw
> my work and said that I didn't need to go to any institution. My work
> was that good, even though I had learned from the General Electric
> manual while in camp. But I wish that I had been sent. I maybe would
> have learned some more techniques.

What today we might consider to have been racial discrimination, Bill looked at as a lucky break. He does not complain about missing the opportunity to become a licensed X-ray technician. He even says that it might have saved his life, because he was appalled at the lack of safety that was provided to X-ray technicians in Stanley Park and other area hospitals. But when Bill talks about his work as a technician-orderly, he also talks about what he saw as both employee and coworker in the hospital's everyday routine:

> When I lived in Stanley Park, I thought of the Stanley Park folks as a
> different species. I don't know how you feel about it, but at that time
> they were all so dignified and educated. They were very pleasant. But I
> found out when I was transporting patients . . . that I did not know the
> whole story. There was a black woman once. I was wheeling her down
> the hall and people were just staring. Their eyes were just popping out of
> their heads. Patients, doctors, staff. I don't know how she was admitted.
> She must have been somebody's maid or something. Another time there
> was a black woman who had broken her hip and she was in the E.R.
> which was right by our X-ray department. She was screaming, "I don't
> want to go to the county hospital!" This wasn't Cook County Hospital.
> See, blacks could be treated in the E.R., but could not be admitted as in-
> patients. There was a black hospital in Stanley Park, but it was just a

plain dwelling. You know, a house. She didn't want to go there because she knew it would be bad. I heard her say, "If they send me there, I'll be dead." That's how bad it was in Stanley Park.

It was bad in Stanley Park for blacks. Bill was sure of that. From the very beginning of his own employment at the hospital he knew that, although he was not being fairly paid, things were much worse for blacks:

I was getting $110 per month and paying $30 for room rent. I would pay for my own meals. Soon after I got there the head of the department upped my pay to $125. But there were women who worked in the laundry who got $60 per month. That laundry work was right above the furnace, so you would get the heat from the laundry and the furnace. If you went in there, you could feel the heat on the soles of your shoes. I don't know how they could stand it in the summertime. There were no windows, and I don't know if it would have helped, with the furnace at your feet. Only black women worked in the laundry, and they would come all the way from the South Side. They would take a bus and then a train and then sometimes another bus and then have to turn around and do the same thing to get home. And they only got paid $60 per month. So I was lucky. I was being highly paid by the hospital's standards.

During the course of working at Stanley Park Hospital, Bill became friendly with a doctor who was a Japanese national. Doctor Nishida had practiced medicine in Japan before World War II and had managed to immigrate to the United States right after the war. He was undergoing his mandatory internship at the hospital when Bill first met him. As two of four employees of Japanese ancestry—the other two men were on work release from mental institutions—Bill and Dr. Nishida got to know each other somewhat. On some occasions the doctor would tell Bill about his time in the army in Manchuria and Korea, and that he had mistreated his servants. After telling me all of this, Bill leaned closer and whispered that there was something else I should know about Dr. Nishida:

After he left Stanley Park, he eventually transferred to Northwestern University Hospital. I guess he got his license. Here he was in the Uptown area and all of a sudden he moved to the South Side. I heard in a roundabout way that the reason he moved to down there was because he could get patients there. You know. Black people. There weren't any Japanese around down where he was, but I heard that down there he was just flooded with patients. He must have been very successful because he eventually moved to Hawaii.

Bill remembers an incident, sometime between 1946 and 1953, when the lines between blacks and whites were redrawn by another group, like Japanese Americans, whose position in the hierarchies was undefined and thus in some ways unsettling:

> Did I tell you that blacks were not allowed to eat in the cafeteria? See, what happened was there was a strike in Indiana and the striking Puerto Rican steelworkers came to work in the hospital because we were short on labor. About a half dozen of them came to work at Stanley Park Hospital. Puerto Ricans are almost black. Dark, but not too dark. So they were not allowed to eat there, either. And you know what they said? They said "OK, if you aren't going to let us eat there, then we will quit!" They were allowed to eat in the cafeteria. After that blacks could eat there, too, if they wanted to. But I asked my friend Mary why she did not start going to eat in there and she said, "No, if they never let us eat in there all these years, then why should I eat in there now?"

If Bill could not turn a blind eye to the discrimination and injustice he saw, he certainly could not ignore what he experienced personally. Whether it was the Polish co-worker who protested when Bill was invited to the department's Christmas party or whether it was the coworker who was "prejudiced against blacks and Japanese" and made cracks to Bill about all Japanese women being whores, Bill remembers the pain of being nonwhite at many of his jobs. But one of Bill's most vivid recollections is going to Chicago's rioted-out areas in 1968. He says: "Well, I went down to the South Side and West Side areas to look around, and it scared me because I felt like a foreigner. Not a single white or Oriental face around. You get that fear. When I visited those areas, I thought that it was better not to stick around. I wanted to see the damage. But [nervous laugh] I took the next train back. Those riots were the reason that I moved back to California for a while."[10] Yet the irony in all this is that these events, which caused Bill to rethink his future in Chicago, paved the way for Al Kawaii to do things that no other Asian American had been allowed to do before.

Bill eventually returned to Chicago after a few months in Los Angeles. "I came back. You can always find a job in Chicago," he says. Neither black nor white, neither professional nor unskilled, Bill gained at Stanley Park Hospital an awareness of the daily inequalities of race that in the end could not keep him away from Chicago. Today he lives in one of Chicago's most multiracial, and most rapidly gentrifying, neighborhoods.

His life is a tale of the "other side" of Japanese American experience. Bill and the others whose words I offer here do seem unimaginable indeed, if we accept preconceived notions of Japanese Americans and race in Chicago. Japanese Americans are not supposed to have taken account of what was going on around them racially, and if they did, they were not supposed to have been angered by what they saw and experienced. Yet race as seen through the lenses of this group of Nisei tells us that there are other stories to be heard—accounts that encourage us to think in terms of larger interconnected histories and patterns and to see the possibility that some Japanese Americans would speak up and act out against what they saw with their "other awareness."

FIELD NOTES

July 28, 1996

Today was probably the strangest day ever. How weird that it is right when I am getting ready to wrap up my work at the Chicago Historical Society. Who knows if it is a self-fulfilling need to see this kind of stuff or if it would have happened anyway? In any case, the best quote ever came from my friend the "old black man" cloakroom attendant. There he was standing in his uniform jacket right in front of the "No tipping" sign posted on one of the racks. He isn't really all that old, but he stands out because he is older than the others—mostly black and Latino "kids" in their twenties. As usual he was chatty, but he asked the question that he had probably always wanted to ask: What I was "doing up there"? I like the way he made "up there" sound like a place that I was lucky to return from. How strange that after all this time he decided to ask about my research. He had always been nicer than that older black woman who takes your ticket or pass at the entrance to the collections. She has never asked me about my research, and she clearly does not like me. Who knows why? I could speculate, but that would not be "professional."

In any case, he outdid himself today with his reaction to my answer, "I am looking for archival materials that talk about Japanese Americans' arrival in Chicago and how blacks and Japanese Americans were used against each other. You know how people ignore the similarities in our experiences." Yow! The look on his face. How can I describe it? His lip curled up and he snarled, I mean really snarled. "Girl, you've been in those books too long. Those people only care about themselves and they sure don't care about me and you. Remember a few years back when they were dumping all those

*cars on us and saying all those things about how they were better than us?
Whenever they come down here in those tour groups, they act all uppity,
getting off those buses. You mean to tell me you have been coming down
here all this time trying to prove that? How could those people ever have
anything in common with us? You don't see them down here working, do
you?" He didn't care to hear my "But, but, I have found lots of evidence" or
"I think you are confusing Japanese Americans with people from Japan."
He looked at me like I was a crazed maniac and a very, very naive, overeducated girl. I guess he and the woman who takes the tickets can have a good
time talking about that crazy one who used to come here all the time. Good
thing I am finished there. I think today may have been my last day seeing a
smiling face when I checked my bicycle helmet.*

CHAPTER FIVE

Give Me Five on the Black Man's Side

Japanese American Activism in Chicago

Give me five. Now gimme five on the black man's side. When I was growing up, my older male cousins not only taught me to give them five but also to give them five on the black man's side. As I learned in the backyards, basements, and front porches of my extended kin in Detroit, giving five on the black man's side was something extra, something special. The black man's side was the back of your hand (where you could *see* your blackness). We all knew the sly hidden secret. We knew that receiving five on the black man's side (your side) hurt. The more gleeful you were to give five on the black man's side, the more pain the receiver experienced. Even at age six the irony in the act of giving five on the black man's side was clear: why would anyone want to be on the black man's side when it hurts so bad?

Who would want to be on the black man's side indeed? When we think of Japanese Americans, we rarely think of them as being on the black man's side. Most of us, whether of Asian ancestry or not, see Asian American activism as nonexistent. The images of standing up and arguing for what you believe in, agitating, or making a stink—we think of none of these things when we imagine the mythical Asian Americans. We believe that they (or we) are quiet and well-behaved examples for all people of color. Despite the recent efforts of Asian Americanist scholars, journalists, and filmmakers, Americans of all hues continue to cling to images of easygoing and overachieving Asians in America. This included me, too, before I conducted my fieldwork. My informants helped me to see that there have been at least fifty years of Japanese American activism in Chicago. These years have often been in solidarity with other non-whites, including the black population in Chicago. And, although when we think of urban activism in Chicago we often think of young white men and women going head to head with Chicago police or of Jesse Jackson's Operation Push demanding services for the poor, the men and women on the Japanese American Citizen's League (JACL) Human Rights Committee are also part of the city's activist core. They are just the latest installment of a half century of Japanese American progressive politics. Granted, my informants, who welcomed me as a full member of the Human Rights Committee (HRC), are indeed special cases, but nevertheless they give testimony to an activism that has consistently moved beyond black and white conflicts, but at the same time has never been limited to "yellow power." Most important, Japanese American activism in postwar Chicago underscores Asian Americanist Omatsu's belief (1994) that the issues confronting Asian Americans—"racism and sexism, economic justice and human rights, coalition building and community empowerment"—are not limited to Asian American communities.

Americans believe, despite contrary evidence, that Asian Americans are not activists. This type of thinking seems so natural because of what activism has come to mean in this country. Resistance and political activity have become synonymous with blacks in Selma, Yippies in Chicago, gays and lesbians marching in Washington, D.C., or Greenpeace takeovers on the open seas. America likes its images to be clear and easy to follow, so black versus white, young versus old, sexual others versus American heterosexuality, and earth lovers versus big business are the struggles that define conflict and activism. There are few accounts of "crossover" coalitions, and they rarely highlight Asian American participation. For the most part, activism in the American public psyche centers around the commonsensical "naturalness" of helping one's own people first, perhaps even exclusively. Because of these two misrepresentations of activism and political struggle in America—that Asian Americans are left out of the definitions of political activity and that self-interest motivates activism—Japanese Americans occupy a strange and ironic place in American activism. Japanese American activism, upon close inspection, betrays these misconceptions.

Japanese Americans fought and won a first in American history—reparations and an apology from the United States for their mistreatment—something that had never been done before or after. The past and present history of Japanese American activism in Chicago challenges common-place definitions of activism and gives evidence of the powerful potential of multiracial and intergenerational coalitions and the people who believe in them. I examine the belief that Asian Americans are culturally opposed to activism of any kind and focus on two moments in the history of Japanese American activism when black and Japanese American interests intersected. In the final section of the chapter, I highlight the ways that the activities of the Human Rights Committee in Chicago challenge the mythologies of Japanese American activism, while at the same time isolating its members from their families, friends, and neighbors. Yet within this isolation is the reality of double-crossing the color line.

It may be too easy to use William F. Buckley Jr. as an example of the kind of assumptions and mythologies that we ingest nationally. As an outspoken conservative, Buckley has long maintained a distaste for activism and social change. Yet his reaction in 1997 to protests over a *National Review* cover that depicted Al Gore, Hillary Clinton, and Bill Clinton in "yellowface" is useful in understanding the spin that is often placed on Asian American activism. What he wrote in response to the nation-wide and week-long protests against the magazine's commentary on the "Asian influence" in the national Democratic Party is telling:

> The grievance industry has an Asiatic division and it is in overdrive against *The National Review* in protest against its cover on the March 24 issue.... [T]hat cover has stirred the ire not of Asian-Americans, who are too levelheaded to transmute caricature into race prejudice, but of defamation-seeking outfits that want to earn their keep. They are hectoring their constituents, pleading them to retaliate against *National Review* by, among other things, protesting to one of its advertisers, Toyota. (Buckley 1997)

Leaving Buckley's racist stereotypes and vocabulary aside, his account of the protests completely misrepresents them. He was wrong. This was not the story of innocent or naive Asian Americans being misled or misrepresented by agitators. Instead the protests speak to what is so often ignored or misrepresented in U.S. public culture—multiracial, multi-generational outrage and a willingness to do something about it. In the first few days after the cover appeared, the calls for rallies and boycotts of the magazine and its sponsors went out over the Internet and were posted in public spaces throughout the country. The rallies that took place over the next few days crossed generational boundaries. In Los

Angeles, Asian American law students joined with Asian American senior citizens. They chanted and pounded their fists in the air at the continuation of racist stereotypes. In New York, groups that did not seem to belong together, if conventional views of political struggle are to be believed, came together in a series of large rallies. And although members of the Asian American Legal Defense and Education Fund (ALDEF) led the New York protests, "the hectors" were not stirred up by the NAACP, the American Jewish Committee, or the AFL-CIO, even though all these groups participated in the open-air protests. Buckley's reading, then, no matter how easy a target, is just one example of the mythology surrounding Asian American activism. We tend to conclude that such activities of crossing boundaries and recognizing mutual struggles are rare and, when they do occur, are the result of outsiders or renegades (see Wang 1998). These mythologies are not the full story of Asian American activism. The facts behind the *National Review* protests and the published account of these efforts not only contradict our mythologies, but also encourage us to rethink what we assume about Asian American activism.

Japanese American Activism in Chicago

What do I mean when I use the term "Japanese American activism" in Chicago? What assumptions do I bring to the notion? Given the changing imagery of Japanese Americans' position in Chicago over the past fifty years, going from near black to model minority, there can be no one definition of Japanese American activism. Of course, the efforts to gain redress are examples, yet they should not be thought of as the defining moment in Japanese American activism, either in Chicago or in the nation. Although the scale and scope of the redress campaign is undeniably an important moment, most Americans read that campaign as an example supporting the mythology of Asian American activism— the idea that when Asian Americans do speak up and organize, it is done in self-interest.[1] There is another way to think about Japanese American activism and the motives behind it. Today the JACL's Human Rights Committee is a continuation of what I see as a powerful tradition, even if limited, of boundary-crossing activism in Chicago.

Since relocation to Chicago began, there have been Japanese Americans who have organized across what are supposed to be impenetrable boundaries in order to protest inequality and discrimination. Two moments that attest to this are 1946 and 1970. During both those years some Japanese Americans, influenced by the hardening rhetoric and reality of racial politics in Chicago and their own changing positions within them, made efforts to organize across divisions. It is also evident that larger forces have worked to dissolve such attempts. This is not to say that there are groups of men and women or institutions that have colluded to keep Japanese Americans from double-crossing the boundaries of race, class, gender, and generation. Yet there are reasons that this type of activism, which challenges conventional myths about Asian Americans, has been discouraged by a variety of interests. The events of 1946 and 1970 underscore the need to evaluate how divisive assumptions about race and activism benefit from the suppression of Japanese American activism.

1946: The Chicago Resettlers' Committee

World War II ended in 1945. Throughout the war Japanese Americans had migrated to Chicago, in part because of the plentiful jobs and growing Japanese American community. Released from Internment camps, finishing college, or returning from the military, Japanese Americans came to Chicago. This peak of Japanese American relocatees coincided with a general slowdown in the national economy. Wartime industries were no longer booming, and the employers who had begged for workers during the war were no longer doing so. Jobs were not hard to come by, but the high wages of the wartime era were not so easy to find. The peak of relocation also coincided with Chicago's notorious housing shortage. It would be years before there would be enough housing, either in the city or the suburbs, for most Chicagoans to be able to pick and choose where they wanted to live and live comfortably. On top of all of this was Chicago's famous brand of racial discrimination. Japanese Americans, whether anyone acknowledged it or not, were starting over in a city with a long tradition in which people of color, especially blacks, faced discrimination in housing and employment. In a city like Chicago, where the social service system was primed to think of race and the need for special support in black terms, Japanese Americans quickly learned that if they wanted to survive they would need to fit into the existing system. With the dissolution of the War Relocation Authority (WRA), Japanese Americans began to form their own organizations designed to help the resettlers in their transition to Chicago. Japanese American leaders began to suggest that the community needed a self-ruled organization to aid Japanese American relocatees.

The Chicago Resettlers' Committee (CRC) was one of two Japanese American organizations in Chicago that acted on the behalf of the resettlers. The other was the local chapter of the national JACL. In 1946 a multiracial group of community leaders and officials began the CRC in anticipation of the closing of the Chicago WRA office. But by the time the organization was chartered in 1947, the CRC's leaders were all Japanese. It should also be noted that the CRC was started in part by those Issei and Nisei who did not want a "political organization" like the JACL, but instead hoped for a social support system for the resettlers. The members of the committee, mostly older Nisei and younger Issei, believed that resettlement had created problems within the community.[2] They believed that the process that had begun during Internment—an upset of the traditional generational balance of power in Japanese households—was continuing in Chicago and had to be stopped. Even though housing was poor and well-paying jobs were limited in Chicago for the majority of resettlers, the CRC's first efforts concentrated on rebuilding Japanese cultural traditions and strengthening Japanese families.

In 1946, in order to get funding and recognition from government and private agencies, the CRC executive board—then made up of white, black, and Nikkei business and civic leaders—wrote a series of reports. In the social analysis report, good housing was seen as a long-term goal for successful resettlement, yet for the immediate future there was an extreme need for "wholesome attractive social programs." The report also reflected a deep concern with a host of social crimes, particularly with fourteen reports of out-of-wedlock pregnancies and a South Side resettler rapist who was still at large.[3] The CRC was worried that these types of "criminal infatia accentuate[d] the community's general dereliction" (CRC 1946). But just a year later, the CRC had made a radical change in the way it framed its needs and the issues that were hindering successful Japanese resettlement.

By April 1947, the CRC was a recognized agency within Chicago's social agency network. In its second annual report, the committee had switched from cultural problems to the restrictive housing covenants that kept Japanese Americans segregated in North and South Side neighborhoods. The CRC leaders concluded that "[f]rom the standpoint of crime, delinquency, and racial tensions... perhaps the least desirable areas of long-range resettlement" had become the principal areas of re-settlement (CRC 1947: 1). Yet in the same progress report, the committee noted that on the "positive side of the resettlement ledger of 1947," there was a high rate of assimilation among Japanese Americans "in their everyday associations with fellow workers, friends, and neighbors. The climate for relatively unprejudiced acceptance of resettlers by white Chicagoans continues, on the whole, to be friendly and fair" (CRC 1947: 3).

What had happened between 1946 and 1947 that might have caused the CRC to change its focus on the problems facing the resettlers? And how was it that now whites were mentioned specifically as positive forces in resettlement, when race had not been mentioned a year earlier? Was it coincidence that the CRC board was now using the term "segregation" to describe why Japanese Americans were in trouble in Chicago? What to make of the fact that they were segregated on the same South Side that blacks were crammed into? Some might argue that these changes were inevitable because Japanese Americans had brought a preference for whites over blacks from the West Coast. Others might suggest that it was only to be expected that Japanese Americans would want to move to neighborhoods with better housing stock and services. I argue that perhaps part of the explanation for what happened was the CRC's place in Chicago's larger social service network.

In the 1947 report, the CRC states that one of the major developments of the previous year was that the organization had become the primary link between Japanese Americans and Chicago's private and public welfare agencies. Certainly Chicago social agencies would have preferred funding community groups that framed their problems to mesh with larger perspectives on race and social services in Chicago. By noting that white Americans were willing and friendly partners in Japanese American uplift, the CRC was able to suggest that Japanese Americans belonged in white society, not black. Japanese Americans were having trouble in Chicago because they were in bad neighborhoods. Their traditional culture was at risk because of their surroundings. But it was not the material conditions in the South Side neighborhoods; it was the cultural conditions—"crime, delinquency, and racial tensions." The unspoken assumption was that it was not whites but blacks who were a threat to successful relocation. In the end, we cannot know for sure what brought about the changes within the CRC; nevertheless, by September 1947, CRC documents had dropped the following statement:

The people of Japanese descent, American citizens and aliens alike, desire to contribute to the strength of the forces of democracy and peace in America. We wish to join forces with all Americans, regardless of race, creed or color, in promoting social and economic progress. (CRC 1946: 1)

The competition for funds between blacks and Japanese Americans during those early months of the CRC's existence helped to define the path of Japanese American activism in Chicago. From the beginning, CRC leaders had made use of more "experienced Negro leaders," who told them how to frame proposals for grants from agencies when they had failed. "Nisei leaders and leaders of other minority groups worked closely together, and Japanese Americans were exposed to the company of the Negro elite, both socially and on 'race relations' business" (Nishi 1963: 228). But at the same time, the group was learning other facts. In 1946, in what may have been one of the most important meetings in the history of Japanese Americans in Chicago, the CRC's representatives met with the director of the Council of Social Agencies in Chicago and were told that they had no business in "special pleading," because "other groups were in far greater need of help" (CRC 1946: 227). According to Nishi, with black leaders seeing a new ally in Japanese Americans, while whites in power were convinced that Japanese Americans did not need colored monies, the CRC, "once adequately informed, [learned] that the rational processes of the established social structure would compensate for the accumulation of special disabilities and the prevention of special hardship" (215). In other words, Nisei leaders decided that Japanese Americans would not practice hat-in-hand activism. They would not be like blacks.

The CRC activists operated in multiracial circles from the beginning and learned that even when concentrating on Japanese American needs, activism in Chicago would have to mean paying attention to blacks as well. They were aware that they were in a place where race mattered and found themselves making decisions (or perhaps having them made on their behalf) about how their activism would be defined by Japanese Americans and non-Japanese alike. It might have seemed to the leaders of the CRC that they had done the right thing, turning away from the organization's early history of crossing racial lines. Over the next fifteen years, Japanese Americans did seem to move from being at-risk resettlers to prospering residents. Influenced by the prevailing political and economic situation in Chicago, the CRC's collective decision to create a

Japanese American activism in Chicago that was nonconfrontational and distanced from black Chicagoans did not stop other Japanese Americans from wanting the opposite. No matter who was making the decisions about what Japanese Americans' connections with blacks in Chicago would be, there was no way to escape the fact that the relationship between the two groups was influenced by each of their respective positions in the city and the nation.

1970: The JACL National Convention and the Black Panther Party

The clichéd accounts of activism in the 1960s almost always include youth of color. Within this mixture of mythologies and realities, Chicago is never left out as an important part of our collective oral history of activism in the United States. But I never would have known to look at Chicago in 1970, at a convention that had nothing to do with presidential elections (but everything to do with how much we don't know about Japanese American activism), if it hadn't been for an interview with one of my informants. Rose Yamamura assumed that I already knew about what she called the "Palmer House Black Panther" murder when she mentioned it in passing one spring day. She told me it had taken place at the JACL convention in Chicago in the seventies and that it had caused a great deal of trouble and sorrow. When I told her that I had never heard of it, she was shocked. She was surprised that no one had mentioned it to me, since by that time I had been conducting interviews for months. Rose believed that this incident was just what I was looking for if I wanted to know about Japanese American/black activism in Chicago. "There was a lot of stuff going on between the Nisei and the Sansei at that time, because the Sansei were planning on staging a strike or sit-in at the main meetings and the Nisei in charge didn't want that. After the murder, it didn't take place, because everybody was so shook up."

On July 17, 1970, two days before my sixth birthday and the first day of the Twenty-first JACL National Convention, eighteen-year-old Evelyn Okuba was murdered in her downtown Chicago hotel room. One of her two roommates, seventeen-year-old Ranko Carol Yamada, was attacked as well but survived, despite being slashed in the throat and receiving multiple stab wounds with a hunting knife. She was able to describe her attacker as a black man. Chicago's press went wild. Both girls had traveled from California to attend the JACL convention, and, as Rose suggested, the newspapers hinted that the girls had been hanging out with black militant groups and had met with the Young Lords, a Latino group, the previous week. Preliminary reports stated that the attacker was thought to be a black man who had stood out at a "youthful discussion group/ rap session" that Evelyn Okuba had attended at the Conrad Hilton earlier in the week. Yet for the first few days after the incident, Chicago papers reported in front-page stories that the motive for the attack had been rape. On July 18, the *Chicago Sun-Times* published an article, "Girl Writes Out Description of Killer in Hotel." In the piece Commander John Carton of the homicide division was quoted as saying that Japanese American convention leaders had assured him that "the youngsters confined their dating to their own group."

The changing explanations and rationales continued. A few days later, in much smaller articles buried deep in the back sections of the newspapers, it was reported that police detectives no longer thought rape was the motive for the attack. In place of a sensational rape-murder, the explanation had come to involve race and dangerous men. Now articles described hotel employees who had seen a "high-afro, dashiki-wearing" man in the Palmer House the day of the attacks.[4]

In the course of researching Rose's lead, I began to wonder why only she had told me about the incident. The sexual and racial politics behind all of it seemed too much, almost overpowering, at the end of my research. I found myself wanting to find Carol Yamada and ask her about the messages she wrote in crayon while she thought she was dying. "Gory, but it really doesn't hurt." "Don't blame him it was not his fault. There must be peace." I wondered if she had continued working with blacks and working with striking grape pickers in California, as had been reported in the newspaper articles.

The killer was never found, although Carol Yamada eventually improved enough to tell investigators that the killer was no one she had ever met. Rose told me about the incident because she thought that this was a moment when Japanese Americans in Chicago had faced collective and individual decisions about the relationship between Japanese Americans and blacks. She believes that most of those who know about the murder still assume that it was the "Black Panthers that did it." No matter who or what was behind the attack, the incident could not be ignored by Japanese American communities. Its ability to squelch the Sansei protest and to continue today in Japanese American oral history as "the Black Panther attack" is indicative of the attack's place in Chicago's Japanese American activism. Just like the CRC's moment of "choice," Japanese Americans in Chicago who read or heard about the murder and attack would have had cause to think about activism in general and building coalitions, especially with blacks. From investigating these two historical accounts, it would be understandable to think that boundary-crossing Japanese American activism would not exist in Chicago today. But this would not be an accurate assumption.

The Human Rights Committee

Like the better-known Japanese American activist, Yuri Kochiyama, Tom Watanabe risked jail when he participated in lunch-counter sit-ins during the civil rights movement.[5] Dan Hayashi might be compared to Kochiyama, too, because like her, Dan is a prominent supporter and activist in the Puerto Rican nationalist movement. For more than twenty years Bill Murasaki has consistently donated time and supplies to local organizations whenever signs and placards are needed for protests. Such work may not seem important in a world where you can be killed for speaking out, but it is, nevertheless. No, the Human Rights Committee members are not the Japanese American activists we hear about, the few times we do hear about them. Unlike Yuri Kochiyama or the No-No Boys, the members of the HRC are not icons of Japanese American activism.[6] But their activism and its centrality to their notions of self-identity are indispensable to any understanding of race and Japanese American experience.

I was able to see two views of the HRC's little-known but vital activism. One view came from what I heard from each member about other members. I soon found out that nobody ever really wanted to offer up his or her actions as examples of activism. When I would ask the "guilty" party if what I had heard was true, each time I would get a humble confirmation, followed by some such comment as "I do what I can, but you should talk to so and so about his/her past." It was the same with all of the HRC members—extreme pride and respect for each other, but humility for themselves. This was perhaps one of the most difficult things for me to accept about my interviewing. I could not escape the feeling that so much was being held back because of humility.

The other view I received came from the almost two years that I was allowed into the HRC. In this case, however, humility about the past changed into excitement about the collective present. It was an exciting time for me. I had rarely been around a group of people of any age who were so intelligent, well-read, and passionate about speaking out against inequality. Although I was often uneasy about my place on the committee as a full voting member, with the power to make decisions about where the committee would direct its focus, I could not help but get excited about the HRC, too.

These two views of HRC activism reflect the ways that the little-known brand of Japanese American activism in Chicago crosses the lines that divide. The HRC members use their past to direct their present in the hopes of influencing what equality, human rights, and boundary-crossing identity will mean to us all in the future.

There is one significant case that I learned about secondhand—an incident known in Chicago as the George Risper case. Like many Chicagoans, I first heard about the case on the night of the incident in 1994. Risper, a black eighth-grade honors student, was waiting with some of his white teammates for their school bus after a basketball game that March night. The school they had just played against was in a predominately white neighborhood. Two white Chicago police officers came by and threw Risper to the ground; as one of the officers began to beat him, his partner stood by and watched. George's teammates tried to stop the unprovoked attack, yet the policemen paid them no attention. Finally a teacher's aide, who was white, convinced the policemen that Risper did in fact belong with the team. Risper was beaten so badly that he was taken to the hospital for treatment. During the weeks following the attack, despite numerous witnesses, the police department attempted to downplay the incident. Chicagoans were angry, black community leaders especially so. Television stations broadcast footage from a series of protests that took place in support of Risper. I saw one station's coverage, the cameras zooming in on an elderly black woman crying as a black man's voice thundered across the downtown plaza. All of Chicago seemed stunned by the act and the police department's attitude.

I began my fieldwork with the HRC not long after the Risper incident. For the members of the HRC, the incident was important. Many of my initial interviews mention the Risper case and the group's participation in the week of rallies and in the legal case against the city. I was

Figure 11. George Risper protest, downtown Chicago.

lucky to have started my fieldwork at that moment. The Risper case illuminated how the HRC worked and also why the members thought the HRC should exist.

Why would Japanese American men and women in their seventies and eighties leave their homes to picket, protest, and donate money to what many in the city believed was another sad but undeniably African American–police–white problem? Al Kawaii's explanation for why he felt so strongly about supporting Risper is useful in understanding why the case is so symbolic.

For Al the incident brought back memories of what happened to a friend during Japanese American relocation to Chicago after World War II:

A friend of mine was on the corner of Clark and Maple. We were living in the Maple Manor at that time. He was with a friend and then another friend came up and joined them. I think that there were only three of them standing on the corner. They were getting reacquainted since they had not seen each other in a long time. But they got picked up by the cops, taken in, and later released only after some time. That kind of thing happened then. I can't tell you how angry I was. But those were the days when you didn't say anything. That is why I got involved with the Risper case, because it still happens today, and you can say something, which . . . you couldn't do back then.

The memories of what it was like "back then" combine with more than fifty years of living in Chicago in the collective HRC mind. In directing their attention to issues like the Risper case, HRC members cross the boundaries that divide—gender, race, generation, class, neighborhood—because of and not in spite of being Nisei in Chicago.

After I was welcomed into the HRC I began to understand how the committee worked—how decisions were made, how disagreements were resolved, and the strange place the HRC occupied within its parent organization. Each month the group comes together at the JACL headquarters in Andersonville. Even though there are officially eleven to fifteen members, usually only six or seven attend any given meeting. There are three Sansei members; the rest are Nisei. With a slight nod to parliamentary procedure, the meetings begin with Dan Hayashi handing out an agenda. Usually one page, it lists the various meetings that members have attended in the past month (and are expected to give reports on), as well as things that Dan or other members feel the committee should discuss. Despite this written plan, most of the time the meetings are free-spirited. Often the meetings veer off course because someone will mention a news item or talk about something overheard in the street. Sometimes the members relate a contemporary problem to what happened to them during relocation. Decisions on which areas to assist, or when the group should organize a protest, or whether or not to join in one are usually made collectively in the monthly meetings, although Dan's suggestions are often unchallenged. Yet there are always debates among the members about whether or not the HRC should be involved in a given situation. The scheduled two hours usually pass quickly.

All the members agree that the organizing forces behind the HRC are Dan Hayashi and Lois Chiaki. Lois, a Sansei born in Hawaii, was my first contact in the organization. Yet, soon after I began attending meetings, Lois stopped attending regularly. She and her husband were in the final stages of adopting a child from Latin America. She would continue to show up on a more regular basis a few months later, but never regained her prominence during the time that I was involved with the HRC. Dan immediately took over Lois's duties, as well as continuing his own. Dan led our meetings, typed our agendas, organized those attending protests, acted as a liaison between the HRC and the larger organization, and even made multiple trips to Japan to help in planning and to participate in an international rally for human rights. Through all of this, Dan was often angry and vocal about the particular injustices that he had heard about, read about, or seen in the month since we had last convened. Like many of the HRC members, Dan always downplayed his activism since arriving in Chicago as a young minister in the early 1950s. Only after speaking with Tom Watanabe did I learn that Dan had been one of the principal people who first called attention to, and organized protests about, the Vincent Chin case in 1982.[7]

Dan has been interviewed numerous times and seemed, despite his overwhelming support of my research, to have little patience for academics. During our first interview, he handed me a copy of a chapter in a book that "a black anthropologist before you came along" had written. The chapter was about him. "You can read that if you want to know more about my life." I was a bit taken aback. While the chapter was useful, I also found myself wondering if Dan had only agreed to being interviewed on principle. Later on, about halfway through my fieldwork, I asked Dan where he thought possible solutions for making the United States a more equitable country might be found. He answered, "Not from all of these social scientists and anthropologists. That's for sure." On the surface, his responses seem anti-intellectual. But I do not think that is the explanation. His responses must be put into context.

Dan is what he calls mini-Kibbei.[8] He was born in Seattle in 1920. He spent most of his early childhood in Japan with his grandparents, until he returned to Seattle when he was seven. His father, who worked for the Immigration Office in Seattle, was a prominent member of the Seattle Japanese American community. Thus Dan's father was one of the first Issei to be arrested after Pearl Harbor. Dan and his sister, who is now a well-known poet, went on to college during the war, and Dan became an Episcopalian minister in Chicago. As the war ended, Dan's father and mother were released and relocated to Chicago. Dan's father went on to become an important member of the Chicago Japanese American community, a powerful figure in the nonprofit sector.

It was coming from such a background that Dan arrived in Chicago and began work in a suburban church where he, his wife, and children were the only people of color for miles. The same housing covenants that kept blacks out kept Japanese Americans out as well. Dan quickly became a "house radical"; the rich congregations that he ministered to in Chicago learned that their minister was an outspoken activist. When he retired from his ministry, Dan brought those same views to the HRC.

After fifty years of working for the poor in Chicago and now among like-minded fellow Nisei who speak and act out, Dan's impatience with the trappings of intellectual studies, interviews, and diagrams is understandable. Yet Dan was one of the most vocal and outspoken of my supporters in the HRC. I know that if he had not wanted me to be there, I would not have been. I think in the end, for Dan and many of the others, I was not just a researcher, but someone who shared their concerns.

The HRC's circle of coactivists is far-reaching. The group sends members to about ten different groups around Chicago, ranging from Chinese Americans to Puerto Rican nationalists to Japanese nationals to multiracial anti-police-brutality coalitions. Interests are not limited to issues that affect just one group or community. During my fieldwork, there was an ongoing effort to develop even stronger ties with organizations concerned with police brutality in Chicago. However, some of the most telling aspects of decision making about where to devote time and energy occur when the HRC stays within the "expected" boundaries of Japanese American identity and allegiance.

When Harry Caray, a local white personality and beloved national sports announcer, made national headlines for his racist remarks about a Japanese national major league baseball pitcher, the members of the committee demanded and received a meeting with television executives. I remember the anger and disgust that the members showed when we met for a special meeting to discuss the matter. There was little debate over whether or not this was appropriate HRC business. Two members took written demands to the meeting and gave them to the executives. They probably played a significant role in the decision on the part of management, Caray's employers, to censure the announcer. In another case a few months later, something entirely different took place. There was a long discussion over whether or not the committee should do anything about a housewife living in Detroit, a Japanese national, who had been accused of murdering her child. The woman had been denied translators, and it appeared that the Japanese consulate was not doing much to assist her. Thus the debate did not center on whether or not the woman needed help, but whether it was politically wise for the HRC to get involved in a defense in which Japanese "culture" was being used in an infanticide case. Bill Murasaki pointed out that the Japanese culture argument had been used by Internment supporters back in the forties. Rose Yamamura countered that this woman, like their Issei parents who were illegally incarcerated during the war, was not an American citizen. Rose argued that the HRC should come to her defense whether she was guilty or not. In the end it was decided that the HRC would not assist this woman unless something new developed. Whether or not this had anything to do with gender is unclear. However, in yet another case toward the end of my fieldwork, the question of Japanese culture and gender and the obligations of the HRC to act came up yet again.

When the Equal Employment Opportunity Commission (EEOC) filed a class-action suit against Mitsubishi Motors Manufacturing Corporation of America, Mitsubishi's reaction to the EEOC's charges of widespread and uncontested sexual harassment at its downstate Illinois assembly plant gained much attention.[9] Media stories linked the company's nonreaction to its female workers' complaints to Mitsubishi's Japanese management. Soon Jesse Jackson and Patricia Ireland, president of the National Organization for Women, called for nationwide boycotts against Mitsubishi. Pickets went up in front of the Normal, Illinois, plant and Mitsubishi dealerships nationwide. As was the case with the Japanese national housewife months earlier, July's monthly HRC meeting centered on what the committee should do in response to the Mitsubishi episode. Everyone agreed that the suit was probably justified, but differed again on whether or not the Japanese culture explanations were accurate. Some members, both men and women, spoke of having been in Japan and experiencing Japanese sexism themselves. Others voiced their reservations about a Japanese American group joining in what seemed to be a revival of the Japan-bashing of the 1980s. One member argued that it did not matter whether or not the company was Japanese, the HRC had to take a stand against sexual harassment. After some debate it was decided that the committee would join forces with the coalition of national organizations involved in the Mitsubishi boycotts and pickets.

The HRC members have created their brand of progressive activism. They recognize that their views and activities puzzle their Japanese American friends and relatives because the members devote a great deal of energy to issues that Nisei seem to have no reason to be concerned about. At the same time they also realize that many other "others," especially African Americans, either ignore or resent Japanese Americans because of their model minority status in this country. With this knowledge, and in some respects because of it, the HRC members continue to practice their activism. They themselves are not certain how their activism should work, but they continue to act, knowing that they are crossing the very boundaries that define their existence.

With Isolation

For Tom Watanabe, the HRC committee has been a place where he could continue his friendship with people who think the way that he does about working for multiracial equality:

> I think that in the name of the JACL we do a lot of work and then if it suits them they pick up on it and claim it as a JACL thing, when it was really us who did most of the work. I think the Iva Toguri D'Aquino/Tokyo Rose pardon was one of those. We did a lot of work on that, and when it finally was passed at annual conferences, the JACL national organization took credit for it. I also think that the redress movement came out of Chicago. At least two of the three efforts were Chicago-based. And until the end, the JACL opposed us. I also think that some of the efforts toward opposing the Vietnam War [started] here in Chicago. They didn't carry the label of the JACL, but members of the JACL certainly took part in that. I guess somewhere along the way we broke away from the mainstream of the JACL membership.

Rose sees the tradition of JACL radicals as having a strong base in Chicago, even if it is not so strong today:

> Believe it or not, the Chicago chapter of the JACL is really the most radical. We were the ones that caused a lot of trouble within the JACL over supporting Cesar Chavez. If you had only seen it! We here in Chicago spoke out against the grape growers in central California during the time when Chavez was asking for support for the migrant workers back in the seventies. We wanted the national organization to pass a resolution in support of the United Farm Workers. Well, the Central California chapters of the JACL actually sent a delegation from California to Chicago to try to talk us out of it. It didn't work. We stood our ground, and the chapters from San Francisco and the Pacific Northwest supported us. That Central Cal chapter is probably the most conservative of all the chapters, because it has a lot of rich Republican ranch owners.

Just as there are certainly progressive members in the Central California chapter of the JACL, there are conservative members in the Chicago chapter. After attending a variety of JACL and non-JACL sponsored events, I began to understand what Rose meant when she pointed out:

"Nobody in our community likes to make waves. There are only a few people who are willing to say anything. They will say a lot of things behind somebody's back, but nobody will confront anybody. You see that among the Nisei in the meetings and the social life. Everything festers because nobody wants to ever say anything." The image of the passive Nisei was always contested at community gatherings that I attended.

Every year, Japanese Americans across the country remember the signing of Executive Order 9066. I have attended three of these events, but the one in 1995 stands out. The remembrance was held at Heiwa Terrace. The crowd of about two hundred people was a mixture of the buildings' residents and Nisei and Sansei from all around the Chicago area. There were a few non-Japanese Americans, but most of them were older white men in military uniform. After a few speeches from JACL members, the lights were darkened for the showing of a documentary film. After watching the video presentation about the Japanese American soldiers who fought in Europe during the war, a vocal contest erupted among the white and Japanese American veterans in the audience and a Nisei woman who was known for her outspoken pacifist views. A few people attempted to mediate between the woman and the soldiers. The "discussion" was eventually halted by one of the ceremony's organizers, and everyone slowly moved to the building's dining area for refreshments. Sitting in clusters around tables full of rice crackers and cups of tea, everyone seemed to be talking about what had happened just before. I overheard someone say loudly that somebody needed to "make that woman shut up with her peace business." Someone else said, "She should be ashamed to say what she did in there." A group of friendly Nisei women at my table even told me to make sure not to interview "that woman."[10] The idea that people should not speak up or stick their necks out, especially in public, is one of the most important components of the mythology of Japanese American activism. As an arm of the Chicago JACL, the HRC is caught in the middle of this mythology. They are part of a neglected but strong tradition of activism in a world where Japanese Americans are purported to have been able to cross the color line because of their cultural traditions of silence.

The JACL question is a central component behind the HRC members' activities. Over the past five to ten years, there has been concern in the national organization about the steadily decreasing membership base. With the youngest Nisei now in their seventies, the JACL faces the natural loss of its largest group of members. But the organization's decreasing numbers also have to do with the politics surrounding its past and its future. For some, the organization will always be remembered for its Nisei leaders who implicated innocent Japanese Americans in the war. For others, the organization's post-Internment involvement in civil rights struggles seems to be beyond the scope of what the JACL should be doing—promoting and maintaining Japanese American culture. Yet for others, represented most strongly by the HRC members, the JACL is too much a social organization, with little emphasis on the civil rights lessons that should be learned from what happened to Japanese Americans during the war. Not every HRC member agrees with that, either.

Tom Watanabe's thoughts on the meaning of the JACL's "bad" reputation represent a more forgiving view of what took place during the war. He sees the JACL question as a lesson to all of us about the psychological tactics used by governments:

> I would say that at this point in history, I can't blame them too much for what they did. We need to forgive the JACL leaders who played the role they were given by the government of saying, "Oh, pick up Mr. Sato." When the war broke out the FBI picked up community leaders, who were Issei. And then after that they would pick up the older Nisei, those who were like twenty-five or so. I was never picked up myself, but what they did was try to get those Nisei to talk. They would ask them for names of people. When they didn't they would pick them up a few days later and ask the same questions again and again. This would continue on and on. So given that the JACL took a stand to do everything to prove our loyalty, under that kind of pressure probably everybody would say, "Well, I want to help." They would name some guys who were not against America. They just wanted to prove their loyalty.

Rose Yamamura is more critical than Tom when she talks about how the JACL should be weighed in light of its past and its role in the present:

> One of my criticisms has always been that the JACL has never been willing to stick its neck out. None of us have been willing to stick our necks out on the issues that we should have been. It goes back to when during the war we didn't want to be perceived as unpatriotic. You can see this today, look at how few of us there are that are committed to the kind of work that we do. During the time that the JACL was struggling here in Chicago in those early years, we had good leadership. Back then there were a lot of like-minded Nisei in the chapter.

During my attendance at the monthly HRC meetings, I noted a consistent sadness among the Nisei at what they see as the "Republicanization" of third- and fourth-generation JACL members. As one committee member said, "I get so tired of those Sansei and Yonsei thinking that they are rich white Republicans." After hearing this numerous times, I decided to make it a central question in my future interviews. There was consistency in the response to that as well. "What do you think will happen to the JACL and the Human Rights Committee after the Nisei generation is gone?" got me laughter every time. But as was often the case when it came to looking for answers to difficult questions, Tom Watanabe's voice stood out from the rest.

I decided to ask Tom about the fate of Japanese American activism. "What do you think is going to happen to the kind of work that you do in the HRC since there are no Japanese American members under the age of forty?" He answered with a clear, yet almost unemotional voice, "Everybody is seeking an answer to your question."

When Tom said "everybody," he was right. Today Association for Asian American Studies meetings are full of sessions devoted to the question of Asian American identity and generational differences. Magazines and Web sites written by and for Asian Americans devote a lot of attention to what is a presumably a well-to-do but young readership. Yet the main concern in many of these papers and articles is how increasing rates of intermarriage will affect Asian American identity. This is not what the HRC members are concerned with when thinking about younger generations. For them the generational issue is about responsibility and social awareness. None of the HRC's members' children married Japanese Americans, but I never once heard any of them voice concern over it. And although I often heard them talking about what it would mean to be one-quarter Japanese American, they always seemed more troubled about national politics than about sexual politics.

I believe that for the HRC members, worry about what will happen in the future is tied to what they see as the younger generation's disregard for their activism. I never saw any outright disrespect from younger JACL members toward the older HRC members, yet Dan Hayashi's observation that the JACL's board of directors considered the HRC an "old geezer's indulgence" did not seem an exaggeration. One example occurred during a monthly meeting of the HRC toward the end of the fiscal year. The first order of business was a brainstorming session to determine the best way to argue for an HRC budget increase from the board of directors. The question was whether or not Dan, as the liaison between the board and the HRC, should tell the board what the increase was for. We all knew that Dan and Al Kawaii had already attended a few meetings of a newly organizing multiracial coalition confronting police brutality. The organization was struggling, and everyone agreed that the HRC should pay the fifty dollars that was requested from supporting organizations. There was much discussion about the composition of the board of directors who would have to approve the budget. The board had increasingly had more Sansei and Yonsei members over the years, as the Nisei members have passed away or retired. There was no easy answer. Someone suggested that Dan just pull his age rank with the younger, more conservative, members. Another complained, "It is crazy that we have to scheme just to get a few dollars." In the end Dan announced with a bit of frustration, "None of this may be necessary, because they will probably give in. You know they treat us like children and think that we are senile." In the end, Dan was correct about the board's approval. He reported at the next meeting that everything had gone smoothly, except for a few predicted questions from the most conservative board members. They had wanted to know exactly what this new coalition was going to do and why it should be of any interest to the JACL.[11]

There are conservative Nisei members on the board of directors. In some ways it is more difficult for the HRC to deal with those of their own generation who think that their efforts are misguided or foolish. Tom observed that the conservatism that has come to be synonymous with Japanese American identity today is not restricted to generation or kin:

> I am disturbed by this California Resolution [sic] 187 in which they are not going to give education and medical care to illegal immigrants. It seems to me that the younger Japanese Americans, Sansei, Yonsei, and maybe even the Gosei [fifth generation], aren't actively opposed to this thing. There is no activity being done by the younger ones. They don't take a stand, neither pro nor con. But it isn't just the younger generations that are doing this. My brother, who went through the camp just like the rest of us, told me that he felt that he *had* to vote for that ultraconservative Pete Wilson for governor of California.

But there is not total agreement about the future of the JACL among the HRC members. Bill shocked me one day when he said:

I think the need for the JACL has disappeared. You know most of the Sansei and Yonsei are well off. The organization was protection at the time that we were having all that trouble, being put into camp and so on. Now we don't have that trouble. It is good to have the newsletter, but they just need to forget that other stuff. I am not part of that circle. I am an outsider. I don't even belong to the JACL, but Tom asked me to be part of the HRC and so I agreed.

Bill's actions seemed to deny this statement. For Bill the JACL should not be in the business of having an HRC. The HRC should exist in some capacity, just not in the JACL.

If their friends, relatives, and fellow JACL members view the members' activities as indulgences, the Chicago JACL Human Rights Committee members have not retired peacefully. As the question of what the JACL should do is fiercely debated throughout the organization, the HRC members continue to believe that their experiences during World War II cannot allow them to turn away from civil rights violations and discrimination. Instead they have simply continued their belief that their experiences during World War II necessitate open protests against civil rights violations. They come to the aid of those who seem to have little support as they remember those who helped or should have helped Japanese Americans during the war. Though isolated, the members view the world through a progressive lens that is not limited to things Asian, American, or nonconfrontational. Rose Yamamura says it best:

Doing what we do, you soon learn what people say. "Oh well, we don't need that kind of organization anymore." To me the JACL and what we do in the HRC is for vigilance. Sometimes as an individual you want to speak out, but you can't. I mean one individual speaking out will not make that much of an impression. But if you have got an organization that is speaking out, then that makes a difference.

Masters of the Double Cross

From the beginning of my fieldwork, I was invited to every meeting and event that the Human Rights Committee attended or organized. I must admit that at first their activism seemed extraordinary. The members were some of the most informed, sophisticated, and progressive people I've ever met. Even in a city like Chicago, with its powerful labor history, their collective knowledge of labor disputes throughout the country was amazing.[12] Most of the group read multiple newspapers, magazines, and Web sites every day—proof that the benefits from changes in technology are not limited to the young. Bill Murasaki supplements his reading of two daily papers with a variety of television news programs, but draws the line at talk shows: "I watch the local news every day and every night. At 6:30 I turn to Channel 11 to watch *MacNeil/Lehrer.* I don't watch talk shows. I used to watch *Oprah.* She means well, but these other shows are too rowdy. Talking about family troubles, sex, and all that. There is enough of that in the world. Why have it on television?" Few people devote so much time to learning the different sides of important questions.

Their critical readings of the politics and economics behind national and international events are smart, funny, intelligent, and concerned. One night after a monthly meeting, as was often the case, the committee members lingered in the building for a while, waiting for one of the driving members to get his car and bring it around for the older members who didn't drive. On this May evening, Tom had promised to give rides to Bill Murasaki and Edith and Lou Kaneda. While waiting, a few of the members began to discuss the 1996 presidential election. Al and Dan started joking with a Sansei man who attended HRC meetings occasionally. Soon all of us were laughing as the men began to imitate the candidates' television ads in which they claimed to be putting the well-being of "our seniors" at the top of their agendas. The Republican Party candidate in his seventies, Bob Dole, was spared no dig. Age clearly was not going to win out over political views. But behind their jokes about the individual candidates, their concern was not so much about themselves as seniors, but more about what would happen if both major party candidates kept the other promises they were making to the American voter—drastic cuts in social programs.

However, as nonwhite residents of Chicago for the past fifty years, the members are not so unusual. Like many of their generation, they have watched as good jobs with paid benefits left the city for points both suburban and international, sans the benefits and living wages. They have seen their neighborhoods change as the gentrification of the Chicago's North Side neighborhoods impedes Chicago's immigrant and migrant newcomers' desire for affordable and safe housing. But the members of the HRC still stand out. The popular trick found among a variety of people—thinking that some other group's problems are not yours—does not please the HRC members. They look at the world around them and believe that it is not a fair, just, or livable place for many of their neighbors. They know this not only because of their personal experiences, but also because they continue to think beyond the standard line or official positions. The members believe that the boundaries and divisions between us, especially those between Japanese Americans and blacks, are complicated and not easily crossed. Yet they also know that these differences, perceived and real, paralyze us and thus protect boundaries from being crossed. Believing and knowing as they do, the HRC members are masters of the double cross.

There may not have been a better catalyst for the HRC members' wanting to challenge discrimination than Internment. You might expect that people who experienced discrimination on the basis of their racial classification would later be driven by examining their memories and comparing them with what others experienced. However, this is not always the case; in fact, it is probably the exception. Yet when Bill Murasaki says, "I think the reason why we do this is because we were put into camp. You want to right the ways that America suffers," it is hard to imagine why that response is so unusual. Without question Interment is the most important factor in everything that the HRC does and how its members make sense of what they do. Tom says:

> Dan Hayashi and I have discussed what happened to us during
> Internment a lot. You know, how our government intimidated us into
> implicating innocent Issei and Nisei. We both believe that these are the
> tactics that all governments use to intimidate their citizens. We need to
> tell that story and link it up with the kinds of things recently that go on
> in places like Iran and here with Cubans and Haitians.

It is clear that the Internment had a lot to do with how the HRC members looked at injustice in the world. In trying to make sense of what had happened to them, their ways of thinking about the layers of power that were behind Internment give them a highly sophisticated view of political power and the need for boundary-crossing activism. For Rose, the Quakers' stance against what was happening to Japanese Americans during World War II continues to be an inspiration for her activism:

> My . . . being part of the HRC for the past seven years comes from my
> being involved with the Quakers. I remembered what they did for us
> during the war. And I said to myself, "Why do we have an organization

like the JACL that isn't even going to talk about civil rights or human rights? I mean are we just going to be out there having inaugural dinners and scholarship luncheons?

But it is not only what happened to the Nisei during the war that is important here. The fact that the Issei generation were denied citizenship and then blamed by the government for not being American enough troubles the members. They remember how their parents were treated as noncitizens and today pay close attention to how noncitizens are treated by the government and the citizenry. Civil rights, race, and citizenship are at the top of the HRC agenda because of this strong feeling that Americans ignore important lessons about discrimination's effects on everyone. Tom feels strongly about this:

> You know, even though the JACL members were intimidated into making stories up to prove that they were doing something on behalf of the war effort, I suppose the FBI agents that were intimidating them were under pressure, too. I imagine that if they couldn't find the ten guys that they had been given orders to find, they were probably denied promotion or something like that. This is how we are divided and used against each other.

Tom's involvement in a local organization on behalf of the HRC also underscores his belief that there is not a simplistic answer of "treating foreigners" right:

> I learned a lot when I attended a few meetings of an organization here in Chicago that was concerned with immigrants. It was mostly Koreans, but there were some Filipinos, some Chinese, and a couple of Hispanics. I didn't see any African Americans. Anyway, the argument the speakers were giving was that the immigrants pay taxes and are law-abiding. That is true. But the whole time I kept thinking that there are a lot of Americans that are here by birth and they aren't helped by the federal government. And I don't think that the people at these meetings realized that. It is a huge problem about what is right and wrong. Is America a land where you can come and be welcomed? Do we as Americans welcome those who are oppressed and living in injustice?

Yet there is not a general consensus among the HRC members about how much attention should be given to what goes on outside of the country. One of the main sources of tension among the members, or rather between Dan Hayashi and the rest of the committee, is how to divide their limited resources and time. They cannot be everywhere at once. One member said after a meeting in which Dan had excitedly told about the event he was helping to organize in Japan on behalf of exploited peoples in Asia, "I know those people in Okinawa that Dan wanted to help suffered, but there are so many things that we should be talking about that go on right here in this country." In fact, Rose says: "What I am most proud of is that because of what we have done some of the people who have been discriminated against here in Chicago have come to us [when they needed] help. We've been able to support them and to try to influence their employers. To me that has been the most satisfying. It is something that you can really relate to because it is close to home."

Looking at the world through the lens of Internment does not produce uniform visions of the future. For Bill, who pays close attention to the news media, the future doesn't look bright. The same forces behind Internment continue to create and nurture painful division:

> Like I say, I don't see much room for improvement. Look what happened in Bosnia. All the Serbs killing the Muslims and all the Muslims killing the Serbs. It's tit for tat. Today's paper. Did you look at that?[Points to front page news story.] It's the Dalai Lama. He says we should have more compassion. But it won't happen. He means well. Whenever they need signs I make them. I've made signs all these years because I think it is one way to help fight racism. One way I can elevate the goodness of this society. By the way, I don't think that it will happen. Not as long as the country exists.

While for Rose, the divisions could go away in the future, even if it does not look that way today:

> When I go to speak at schools I see the young people sitting at different tables. You know, the Asians all sit together, blacks sit together, and so on. But on the other hand, I think that there is a lot of intermarrying going on, and slowly but surely things will change. There will always be problems, and if it isn't one thing then it's another, but I am optimistic.

Whatever their views of the future, the HRC members concentrate on the present, with a view that the divisions among people of color in the United States must be crossed if they foster inequality and discrimination. The racial divisions in the United States today inspire the members to double-cross and rework color lines whenever they can.

On the Black Man's Side

At a time in the United States when the idea that discrimination can only exist when there are outward bad feelings and actions involved, Tom's account of what happened when he was asked to participate in a research study on discrimination is an important one:

> A while back some guy from the University of Chicago got my name. He was doing a study on segregated housing. He was asking me questions about how I felt about segregated housing and if I felt that by opening up housing to Asians . . . we were breaking down barriers. I told him, "Yeah. Asians do well with all of that role-playing." [Laughs.] But seriously, I think that it's a reality. If discrimination is ever going to end, then housing has to be desegregated. This researcher told me that those were his findings. But it is all dependent. For example, if they had a study like that in San Francisco and you asked somebody, "Would you rather have a Hispanic or an Asian as a neighbor?" and they said "I would rather have a Hispanic," that would be a big kick in the ass for Asians who think that they are already . . . already . . . So we have got to get a bigger feeling of the practice of discrimination in housing, not just who receives the warmest welcome from his new neighbors.

Tom looks at housing and segregation through a complex lens that places Asian Americans at the center, but still makes the connections with other nonwhites. Tom's involvement in the school board in 1985 also underscores how much he distrusts the popular symbols behind Americans' thinking and speaking about race:

> I won by a big margin. I looked at people. They said, "He's a veteran. OK. I'll vote for him!" [Laughing.] I thought that I could be of help to the community. During that time I attended a lot of meetings, and as council members we were allowed to bring up things like busing or the kinds of courses to teach or whatever. I went to one of these meetings on busing. And I remember I came out of it saying even that select committee had concluded that busing is not the answer. A meeting on busing ended up being about housing and jobs. To this day I believe that to be true. If people get to know each other, that is one thing of course, but busing them away isn't the answer. Those children need parents with decent jobs and housing, and that is what is really the problem of segregation. It is a shame that we spend so much time talking about values and stuff like that. It is a way to avoid the basic issues.

The question of how close to other people of color the HRC members imagine themselves to be is a complicated one. Although each member feels strongly about his or her Japanese American identity, each member also sees Japanese Americans' place in the United States as connected to that of other nonwhites. Bill, with his historian's love of detail and fact, asked me:

Have you heard the expression "a Chinaman's chance"? . . . Back in the 1850s or so, Chinese used to be strung up by the light poles. A lot of that took place. Why? Because when the Chinese first came here they were welcomed because they needed that labor to make the transcontinental railroad. And they needed help, but after that was over they just tried to squash 'em. And after the prejudice against the Chinese, the Japanese came over and they were treated the same way. And after the Japanese, the Filipinos were mistreated, too. Now today the Filipinos that come here are highly educated. The United States took control and educated them, but if you look at Puerto Rico it is very different. The United States took control there but they don't educate them. The people who come here only have a third- or fourth-grade education. That isn't right. When Puerto Ricans come here they are still Spanish in culture. And that is sad, because Puerto Ricans are hardworking people.

It would not be fair to call what the HRC members feel sympathy. It is not so much sympathy as it is a strong conviction that there is something wrong about the way that people of color are played against one another or become convinced that it is in their best interests to ignore one another's histories. Tom Watanabe's perspective on how Internment linked Japanese Americans to Native Americans is an example of the HRC members' perspectives:

You know that during the war the Poston, Arizona, camp was built on reservation land. The federal government gave it back to the Indians after the war relocation was over. So the Indian Council gave its permission to dedicate a monument a while back. And so there was a ceremony to dedicate this monument. A chief went up to the podium and said, "Congratulations, all of you, for being released from your Internment. I wish Indians were." You know they've been there on that reservation for over 165 years? It was a very powerful thing to think about. And then a spokesman for the Nisei said, "We are now challenged to help other oppressed people. We just can't celebrate and say, 'Oh, I'll give this money for our monument in the desert.'" I think that most of us Nisei faced discrimination during the war, and African Americans, Indians, and Hispanics continue to face this kind of discrimination based on race. It has a lot to with attitudes, and it isn't just Caucasians.

Al Kawaii has thought about how the lines are drawn among minorities as well. For Al, Japanese Americans and Native Americans are unwisely factored out of American assumptions about race and are ignored with regard to affirmative action. Contrary to those who think that Asian Americans have crossed the color line, Al believes that they have not and that with such an image they are being doubly discriminated against:

> We have benefited from the civil rights movement. When they started affirmative action, they wanted to get minorities into certain schools and jobs. Within that, Asians became the preferred minority, followed by Hispanics and then last, African Americans. But it does bother me somewhat that when we talk about affirmative action, . . . for the most part people just think in terms of black and brown. And they forget about Asians. Come to think of it, the people that never get mentioned are the Native Americans. I can remember the Bakke case, and it seems to me that it was decided then that affirmative action would be for blacks and Hispanics. Asians would just have to compete with whites. That didn't strike me as right. Because in my way of thinking, we are a minority within minorities. We just get left out.

The members of the HRC believe that they are people of color and that, by virtue of Internment and reparations, Japanese Americans occupy a unique place in U.S. race history. But the members do not imagine themselves as saviors or even role models for minority groups. Instead, by believing that Japanese Americans and blacks have a mutual interest in what happens to each other, the HRC members continue to keep up the hope that others will see the possibilities for a Japanese American–black coalition.

Throughout my fieldwork, as I got to see and learn more about the HRC, I began to wonder and ask about what the members thought of the intermittent attempts to gain reparations for the descendants of slaves in the United States. Tom told me that "nobody can work on behalf of somebody. The victims have to go for themselves. Given that, there is some . . . it isn't publicized too much, but there are exchanges of strategy about how best we can do this." The responses varied from Tom's vague yet positive answer to Rose's thoughts about how difficult it would be for blacks to win reparations today because of the current antagonism in the country to anything dealing with social justice and social programs:

I think that it would be a hard battle for African Americans to win a reparations battle. There were times when we all worked together in the civil rights movement. We learned from each other. We helped each other. I remember the early days here in Chicago when Jesse Jackson was here. Some of us Japanese Americans used to go to meetings. I believe that was one of the times when a lot of civil rights groups were coming together, and I don't know how it came about that we were there. But I remember going to many meetings. I think it depends on the leadership any time that type of thing goes on. Somebody has got to push people.[13]

However, Rose is someone who pushes. Her work in the Chicago public schools, giving presentations to high school students about the implications of Internment and redress to every American, and not just Japanese Americans, has allowed her to come to the conclusion that blacks do not hold any special love for Japanese Americans, just as many Japanese Americans hold deep prejudices against African Americans:

I think that what we went through during Internment for many black people seems insignificant, because of their own history. I think that there may be some animosity. I get it the most from the young educated people who don't really understand what the issue is. For example, I went to Farragut High School to speak, and it is about 95 percent black and Hispanic. So I did what I normally do at these high school talks. I spoke about Internment and reparations. In the question-and-answer session at this huge assembly, a black man who I assume was a teacher stood up and said, "Why should we care about you and why should you get money from the government? You have enough money to buy up all the property."

Rose has also been asked to appear on Chicago's black radio station, WVON, a few times. There, too, she found that many blacks simply could not or would not distinguish between Japanese nationals and Japanese Americans. None of the callers seemed willing to believe that there were similarities between blacks and Japanese Americans:

Some of the things that people said were unbelievable and pretty nasty. But I enjoy that kind of challenge. To me it is an opportunity to educate people. If you don't respond to these things, you just let it continue to grow. I don't like going to a place where everybody agrees. I was there to try to educate people and to make them understand what it is that we are talking about. Wherever I go to do these talks, I try to stress that this is an American issue. It is not a Japanese American issue.

The HRC members are not on the "black side." Yet they are not on the Japanese American side of the color line, as it has been stereotypically defined, either. The notions of "our problem" and "their problem" that are implied in American public culture do not sit well with the HRC members. They are not willing to ignore what they know we all should have learned from Internment. Clearly the mythology that Asian Americans only do for themselves if they do anything at all is clearly incorrect. Yet even as the HRC members continue to defy the images by creating their own brand of activism in Chicago, they are concerned that the memories of the racial injustice that spawned Internment and that fuel their determination will die out with them. They are afraid that the mythologies will come true.

Afterword

Whether or not his mother's story is true, Bill Murasaki's wish that he could hire someone to find out more about what he had not been willing to believe until long after his mother's death serves as both a warning and a call for changes in the study of race in this country:

> If I ever win the Lotto and have some money to spare, I'd like to hire some scholar to look into how Leland Stanford killed Japanese Americans. My mother used to tell me stories about Japanese living in California who worked for Leland Stanford. They wouldn't get paid. When they asked for their back pay, he would have them dynamited. I don't know how many. I never believed my mother until years after she had died. A Japanese American doctor who was treating my bronchitis here in Chicago told me the same story. He had heard it from his father, who was one of the oldest people in camp. The doctor's father had heard it from his father. That's when I decided that my mother was right, and I wished that I had gotten more details from her. I just didn't want to believe that a white man could be that evil. You look up to the white man. It is men like that who years after doing these evil things become world famous as benefactors of mankind. Yet what rogues they are. Leland Stanford must have been a Christian, and no Christian should do that. But then Christians had slaves. Thomas Jefferson had slaves and he had children by his slaves. I just wish I had paid more attention to my mother. I regret that I didn't pay more attention to my mother.

We have much to learn and relearn about the articulation of race in America and about Japanese Americans' changing positions within that articulation. The contradictions that are inherent in Japanese Americans' place in our racial hierarchies and how these disjunctures are mediated in everyday life are central to both twentieth-century and twenty-first-century racial politics.

Du Bois's prediction about the color line and people of color in the twentieth century was accurate. Japanese Americans and blacks have been in competition with each other in the United States for a very long time. The nature of their relationship has changed constantly, but most recently, over the past twenty years, it has become one of immense contrast between the groups. But if there is one common theme that links the past and present of Japanese Americans and blacks, it is how central their relationship has been to the continued power of racial politics. A variety of government policies, media depictions, business interests, community organizations, and race theorists have helped to create, made use of, or made assumptions based on the idea of a Japanese American/black relationship—even if today the assumptions are not openly discussed or recognized. Some Japanese Americans have recognized the competition between themselves and other people of color (especially blacks) as divisive. These men and women have struggled to defy the divisions among people of color that Du Bois believed were integral to the political and economic realities of life in the twentieth century. Indeed, from the beginnings of the relationship on the West Coast to its contemporary dimensions in Chicago, the Japanese/black color line has been as much about the two groups' struggles for equality as it has been about Americans learning to see race primarily as a black/white issue.

As is made clear by the convenient absence of the work of the three Japanese American UCDS students in our contemporary theoretical conceptions of race in America and in Chicago, the connections between Japanese Americans and blacks go unnoticed exactly because they threaten to topple our faith in and understanding of the articulation of race in the United States. Ironically, our collective understandings of civil rights in this country are embedded in the ability to draw clear lines of difference between Japanese American and black approaches to political equality in American politics. We need to confront the suppression or denial of the fact that the black/white race model has been used to keep various groups of color at odds with each other, even in the age of transnational corporations and identities. I believe that one of the most important contributions this book makes to the study of race in the twentieth century is its series of contradictions to the belief that the lines between people of color are rigid and rarely crossed, even in current struggles for political and economic identity. In fact, Japanese American/black connections are at the center of the development and continuation of popular opinions and public policies about race in this country. But they go unnoticed, even when individuals and groups of individuals like those in the Human Rights Committee give testimony to how wrong we are not to take notice.

In light of what the life histories of the HRC members indicate about the issue of the interrelationship of Japanese Americans and race, we have to ask, What is our focus when we think about race in America or try to understand Japanese Americans' history? Why are the dominant pictures of race in black and white, although we know better? Why do our understandings of Japanese American history ignore the place of Japanese Americans in multiracial America? Why do we ignore the possibility that Japanese Americans would know how race works in this country and might dare to challenge how race in America makes life unfair and unequal for nonwhites? Both the focus of our attention and the questions we ask must change if we are to develop an understanding of "race" in struggles for equality.

But this is not just a question for studies of race. We need to challenge widely accepted categories in other areas as well. Cohen (1994) argues that anthropologists approach old age in one of two outdated ways— either as disconnected from the "everyday relevance of the macrosocial world" or as ritual and mythology (145). Cohen maintains that anthropologists need to rethink what kinds of answers they expect from studying the aged. He suggests that geroanthropology must go beyond being a service industry for the bureaucracies of aging, such as nursing homes and convalescent centers. I believe that Cohen's observations are important here. It is not just because most of my informants were over seventy years old. It is because Cohen raises the issue of how the production of knowledge in deeply rooted fields of study and cultural beliefs, such as "old age" or "Asian American history," can become stymied by well-intentioned producers.

Cohen believes that turning the study of the elderly on its head is difficult work, in part because of the undeniable reality that growing old in fact sometimes does mean poverty, isolation, and depression, especially for people of color. However, these are not the only ways that we can or should think about what ethnography among the aging can tell us about history, ideology, and power. This is not to say that every study of aging worth its funding should make links to Foucauldian notions of power in senior centers or question whether or not life truly is poor, solitary, nasty, brutish, and short after age sixty-five. For the aging Nisei members of the HRC, growing older has only strengthened their individual and collective belief that their experiences during and after World War II have given them a special obligation to speak out against the violation of civil rights in the United States and abroad. And although they, like W. E. B. Du Bois, continue to be active into their seventies and eighties, what they most fear about their aging is that their ways of thinking about what it means to be Japanese American—an identity that is strongly connected to the history of civil rights and discrimination against people of color—will die out when they do. It is findings such as these that confirm Cohen's belief that a study of "the elderly" does not have to center on common questions about aging, but must connect them to the larger world. The findings indicate, too, that political and economic inequality cannot be understood through white/nonwhite models alone.

As I have suggested, Cohen's challenge to rethink the treatment of old age in anthropology is also important to understanding this work's relationship to the future of urban anthropology, Asian American studies, and race studies. Here, too, the results suggest that those who study race must change the way they frame their research. Do the anthropological studies of U.S. urban life that center on blacks and whites and that isolate Asian American groups (both recent immigrants and longtime citizens) in an Asian/white world limit the questions and results they provide? Are those results the reality, while what this study presents, an interconnected and powerful relationship between Japanese Americans and blacks in U.S. race culture, is simply a case of statistical outliers? Why do Japanese American elders center their memories, understandings, personal experiences, and desires on fighting antiblack racism in stereotypical images of crime, violence, and dangerous manhood? I would counter that urban anthropology, Asian American studies, race studies and, of course, geroanthropology in the United States must acknowledge that this research is not an isolated picture of events or of extraordinary life histories. Anthropologists who want to know more about race and the culture that nurtures it must acknowledge that local and national political economies work with and often against dominant models of race and racial categorization, and in some cases individuals who are thought to be outside the models are exactly at the center of a better understanding of how race works. Asian Americanists who justifiably see a problem with black-centric studies of race must pay more attention to the interactions between the many Asian American communities and other peoples of color. I hope that my findings are part of a trend to move the study of race in the United States away from insularity and complacency and to expand the ways in which scholars across various disciplines can ask and answer questions about struggles for equality and racial identity among Americans.

The connections between Japanese Americans and blacks have been worked and reworked in Chicago and thus in America, but have not really changed in their importance to the articulation of race in this country. These relationships continue to shape the connections of individuals, organizations, and public culture to race, even when the relationships no longer occupy center stage. But time does not become more complex as it goes on. Its web does not become more intricately or finely spun. We should follow Bill's lead and pay more attention to matters that seem to contradict our understandings of reality before we, too, experience regret.

Like no other group in the United States, perhaps, Japanese Americans have been to the mountaintop and back again. America has been inclined to both love and hate people of Japanese descent. When the first waves of Issei began to arrive on the U.S. mainland in the 1890s, the South was twenty years out of Reconstruction. The Chinese Exclusion Act of 1882 and the Dawes Act of 1885 had recently been passed. These acts and events, although separate, shaped the experiences of all Americans and figured negatively on those of color. Even then, America's promises of democracy and freedom had already been filtered through decades of dealing with the injuns, nigras, heathen Chinee, and little brown brothers when the Issei arrived. Japanese immigrants could not have escaped being raced and placed, even if they had chosen to live in isolated enclaves. They and their descendants would never be able to escape being part of the color line.

Although the men and women of the Human Rights Committee usually downplayed their participation in multiracial coalitions, we all knew that our committee was a rarity in Chicago. If nothing else, a black woman in an organization of Asian American elderly activists probably crossed stereotypes that have some grounding in reality. That reality, in Chicago and most other urban areas in the United States, is that it is difficult to cross the many years of racial, class, and ethnic divisions that have come with struggles for equality in housing, employment, education, and civil rights. Yet the committee members made it a point to search out opportunities where they could prove that it could be done and that such work was extremely important within Chicago's activist community.

My informants tell the nation and the world that Japanese Americans should care about the civil rights of blacks, Latinos, and Southeast Asians. But within the debates and depictions of race relations in the United States, the men and women of the HRC are not supposed to exist. American racial minorities have, by necessity, had to play the system for all it is worth. It is not by innate greed, I think, but more because it is the way that we survive as best we can. I too learned as a child: Why pay attention to *them* when *you* either have or had it so bad? We learn it from our textbooks, from our peers, and of course from our families. In a city like Chicago, this credo is the unspoken teaching of living as a person of color, regardless of class, gender, or age. And despite recent calls for multiculturalism and the subsequent attacks on it by those on the right, we still continue to think of "our" people in rigid frameworks. As long as we continue to say "us" and "them," the color line (and all the other lines of demarcation that give us our identities and shape our lives) will continue to belt the world.

Notes

Preface

1. We were lucky enough to be one of the last groups allowed inside the newly constructed Jüdisches Museum building before it was closed to visitors, from the summer of 2000 to fall 2001, so that the museum's installations and exhibits could be set up.

1. Double-Crossing the Color Line

1. Examples of what seems to be an ever increasing number of black/white race books written for both popular and academic audiences include Barrett 1999, Raybon 1997, Shipler 1997, Sleeper 1997, Steinhorn and Diggs-Brown 1999, and Thernstrom and Thernstrom 1997.

2. My work is thus part of a resurgence of interest in Du Bois and is an expanded look at his enormous insight about and influence on racial tensions and relations in the United States (see Reed 1997; Bell, Grosholz, and Stewart 1998; Katz and Sugrue 1998).

3. Taking a survey of the abundant research on Chicago's ethnic and racial history, one can certainly see that the black/white relationship is given priority. In some ways this is to be expected, because of the reality of the continuing legacy of slavery and antiblack racism in the United States. Yet it is clear that blackness, or the "African American studies equals race studies" approach, exists in many researchers' minds today. See, for a sampling of the ways this plays itself out, A. Hirsch 1995, E. Hirsch 1990, and Holli and Jones 1997.

4. Besides Park 1995, 1996, and 1997, also see Abelmann and Lie 1995; Chang and Leong 1993; Gooding-Williams 1993; Kim, Yu, and Smith 1997; K. Kim 1999; C. Kim 2000; and Yoon 1997 for similar accounts of black-Korean tensions.

5. Prashad 2000 and 2001 are excellent examples of the "new wave" of Asian American studies that goes beyond Korean/black relations. Prashad also is inspired

by Du Bois and presents the historical and contemporary power in the Desi/black relationship. Wu 2001 is also concerned to some extent with Asian Americans' relationship with African Americans. Gallicchio's focus (2000) on black Americans' relationships with both Japan and China prior to World War II is technically considered a contribution to African American studies. But it too reflects the ongoing changes in both Asian American and African American studies. Relatively recent "classics" that look at Japan or Japanese immigrants through the lens of black Americans include Allen 1992, Hellwig 1977, Kearney 1991, and Shankman 1982. Loewen 1999 is yet another classic that contains an important view of black Americans through the lens of Chinese in Mississippi in the early to mid-twentieth century.

6. Yu 2000 focuses on Asian American researchers and students in the twentieth century at the University of Chicago Sociology Department. Yu argues that their presence and research was an important component in the development of the term "Oriental" and its place in contemporary intellectual thought.

7. The coining of the phrase "model minority" is a continual topic of debate for race scholars. There seems to be some confusion about when the term first appeared and who coined the phrase. But there is more than the question of "when and who." What I am asking here is "What confluence of forces across time and space prepared the way for the term to be born?" I believe that an overlooked but significant contribution to the birth of the model minority mythology was what took place in Chicago for the twenty years following World War II, when Japanese Americans began to relocate and challenge the black/white color line.

8. Lee 1999 is an excellent study of the always shifting, but always powerful, images of Asian Americans in U.S. popular culture.

9. See Ichihashi 1932, Matsumoto 1993, and Takaki 1990 for varied approaches and analyses of the effects of anti-Japanese discrimination on first- and second-generation West Coast Japanese Americans.

10. Rydell's work (1984) on the politics and imagery behind world's fairs and expositions is important to note here. It shows just how much Japan's role at the Columbian Exposition in 1893 was tied to the nation's attempts to show itself to the world, but especially Europe and the United States, as a nation to be reckoned with and not a nation to be colonized. Harris 1990 does a similar analysis of the Japanese government's exhibits at world expos and their ties to Japan's struggles to be considered a major world power.

11. Some of this work has reexamined how Franz Boas, W. E. B. Du Bois, St. Clair Drake, Oliver C. Cox, Hortense Powdermaker, and others played critical roles in race theory and United States anthropology. Harrison 1988, Harrison 1995, and Liss 1998 are examples of this turn. As well, di Leonardo 1998 and Mukhopadhyay and Moses 1997 have looked at more recent treatments of race by anthropologists.

12. Prashad 1998, although not addressing anthropology specifically, points to the shift among neoconservatives who have gone from race to culture-based theories to explain economic differences among Americans. Prashad suggests that this shift has complicated the ways that those who want to end racism are able to conduct counterattacks against neoconservatives' views.

13. In general, although there have been numerous studies of Japanese Americans from a variety of disciplines, anthropologists have paid little attention to Japanese Americans and even less attention to Japanese Americans in Chicago. Seminal works that focus on Japanese Americans include Broom and Kitsuse 1973; Daniels 1978;

Glenn 1988; Hatamiya 1993; Matsumoto 1993; O'Brien and Fugita 1991; Tamura 1994; Thomas, Kikuchi, and Sakoda 1952; and Weglyn 1976. Key anthropological texts include Caudill and DeVos 1956; Storn 1986; Takezawa 1995; and Yanagisako 1992. One of the few anthropological studies of Japanese Americans in Chicago is Gehrie's dissertation research (1973) among Chicago's Sansei population.

14. Roediger 1991 has been a key work in the development of my ideas about Japanese Americans and blacks. His influential argument about the psychological and economic rewards of "whiteness" at the turn of the nineteenth to twentieth century made me think about the possibilities of looking at "coloredness" in similar ways.

15. Okihiro 1994 is an extremely important contribution to the study of race and to the development of Japanese American/black race politics theory. Okihiro makes the historical linkages between Asians and Africans in America central to his argument that Asian Americans and blacks have been used against each other. He argues that fluctuations in the economy, constantly shifting ideals of political agency, and the rhetoric of white, not white, and near white have served to widen the gap between the rich and the poor throughout American history. Okihiro's notions of Yellowness and Blackness and how the few degrees of separation between them perpetuate discrimination against nonwhites inspired much of what I do throughout this book.

16. Despite limiting "color" to blacks and whites, Goldfield 1997 searches for the specifics surrounding the interplay between race and class in United States history. According to Goldfield, what exists today is an American workforce that has learned to care little about organizing politically across lines of any sort, but especially racial ones. Also see Sakai 1983 for another analysis of race and class in U.S. history and how the relationship has helped to suppress large-scale political action.

17. The history shared by Japanese and blacks of employment as domestics has yet to be analyzed. The turn-of-the-century Japanese "schoolboy," in many cases a grown man, who performed domestic labor in white households evolved into the Japanese houseboy or gardener preferred by West Coast whites in the 1950s. Japanese American women became stereotyped as nursemaids and domestics well into the late twentieth century (Glenn 1988).

18. From 1901 to 1910, 129,797 Japanese immigrants arrived in the United States (Spickard 1996). This was the decade of the largest number of immigrants from Japan. During the same decade the number of blacks living in West Coast cities increased, albeit slowly (Taylor 1998). By Taylor's estimates there were only about 16,360 blacks living in major West Coast cities in 1910, and according to Spickard's research only around 11,000 Japanese living on the West Coast.

19. Much of what makes up Japanese American studies today centers on the Internment of Japanese Americans, the noted efforts of the 100th Infantry Battalion and 442nd Regimental Combat Team made up of Japanese Americans during World War II, and most recently the redress and reparations movement of the late 1980s.

20. Greenberg 1995 addresses the reasons that Jewish and black civil rights organizations did not do much to protest the War Relocation Authority and its mission to remove, impound, and ultimately relocate much of the West Coast Japanese population. Greenberg believes that although civil rights groups were just beginning to realize that "alliances brought greater clout to any civil rights challenge," most of them ignored the racism behind Japanese American Internment.

21. Takezawa 1995 is certainly one of the most detailed and descriptive accounts of the redress movement to date. While Hatamiya 1993 is similarly strong, it focuses on the legal implications of H.R. 442. Houri 1988 provides an alternative view of the redress movement. Houri, one of the earliest participants in the redress movement, takes issue with how the redress campaign was presented to the American public. His group, the National Council for Japanese American Redress (NCJAR), was based in Chicago and took a more aggressive approach toward gaining redress than did the JACL.

22. I know that I am on dangerous ground here. With redress as the new defining point of Japanese American ethnicity, it has become popular among some legal scholars who practice critical race theory to view the Civil Liberties Act of 1988 as evidence that Asian Americans are affected by a different type of discrimination, one based more on citizenship than on race. Such arguments and distinctions are not limited to legal scholarship. Asian Americanist scholars have pointed to the differences between and among Asian Americans with regard to citizenship and legal status. This emphasis can also be seen more generally in the work of Lowe (1996). Although these distinctions are very real, the lines between race and citizenship are not always clear. As evidenced by the divisive logic and statements from lawmakers and community "activists" that have come out of the Civil Liberties Act of 1988, extreme caution must be taken in thinking about making citizenship and not race a focus in Asian American studies.

23. Jaimes's anthology (1992) is an excellent collection addressing contemporary problems facing Native American communities and their struggles with federal and local governments.

24. *National Geographic* has shaped the way at least two generations of white Americans think about themselves in relation to nonwhite people. Through the national publication's editorial choices, the magazine's depictions of nonwhites in Africa, Asia, and South America have changed to reflect its readers' understandings of American international and domestic events and policies (see Lutz and Collins 1993).

25. The details surrounding *Scene* magazine are sketchy. I first found out about *Scene* through the curator of the small Chicago Japanese American Historical Society. He had four copies in his collection. I then found two more tattered copies in the Chicago Historical Society archives. It is unclear how long the magazine was in publication. All of my informants had either heard of or subscribed to the magazine, but no one was able to remember exactly when it began and when it stopped.

26. Berlant 1997 centers on questions of citizenship and immigration in the United States presented in the national media at the end of the twentieth century. Berlant's work on special issues of magazines illuminates the value that the relationships between Japanese Americans and blacks have in larger arguments about the United States' racial future.

27. In June 1993 the publication's installment in the Asian American series showed a different side of the Japanese American/black connection. "Racial Change Takes to the Suburbs" stressed that Asians were the fastest-growing group of minorities in Chicago's suburbs and faced poverty and discrimination similar to that faced by other minorities, but it highlighted the differences in white suburbanites' response to Asian and black newcomers. What is interesting in this article is how it replicates

what is seen by many as the privileging of Japanese Americans over other Asian groups. Even though the article was about poor and non-English-speaking minorities' fates in Chicago suburbs, Japanese Americans were quoted extensively as Asian American authorities.

2. An Embarrassment of Riches

1. These research objectives were an extension of my work (Harden 1997) on race, gender, and Japanese national identity.

2. Contrary to the image that many Americans might have of the Japanese business executive and his family living in the United States, this group of restaurant service workers shared small cramped downtown studio apartments with up to three other people. In both their working and living conditions, they seemed to have more in common with undocumented workers from Latin America than with their salaried co-nationals living in affluent suburbs or downtown luxury apartments.

3. Although Chicago has seventy-seven official neighborhoods, these neighborhoods also have many more unofficial sections or districts. So although technically I lived in Edgewater, it was unofficially Andersonville. I found that the constantly changing boundaries and names that accompanied the Far North Side's gentrification during my years there created a great deal of confusion among residents, business owners, and politicians. See Williams 1988 for an account of how disagreements over the name and definition of a Washington, D.C., neighborhood were fueled in part by the conflicts between longtime working-class black residents and white urban professional newcomers.

4. Unless otherwise noted, the statistics I use here are from the City of Chicago Department of Planning and Development's *Social and Economic Characteristics of Chicago's Population* (1992).

5. These housing statistics are taken from the Greater Chicago Web site (http://www.greaterchicago.com). These sizable increases have continued into the 2000s.

6. Gitlin and Hollander (1970) detail the lives of white Appalachian migrant workers and their attempts to organize a tenant rights union in Uptown during the late 1960s.

7. Census 2000 results show slight decreases for whites (57 percent), blacks (17 percent), Native Americans (.45 percent), and Asians (12 percent). The categories in the 2000 census that have had increases are "other" (.35 percent), Pacific Islanders (.16 percent), and "multiracial" (4 percent).

8. See Hosokawa 1982 and Spickard 1983 for views of the organization's history that present a more conservative picture of the JACL than what I experienced among my informants.

9. NCJAR filed a class-action suit in federal court while the JACL concentrated on lobbying in Congress. NCJAR openly criticized the JACL for being too easygoing and not wanting to cause trouble in their approach to redress. In the end it was the JACL proposal that was successful (Houri 1988).

10. Although I have kept to my promise of giving my key informants aliases, each of them felt that aliases were not needed. I, however, did not feel that I should use their real names, even though it is true that it would not be difficult to find out

who they are because of their prominence in Chicago. At least three of them have been the subject of local media attention and are well known in Chicago's Japanese American communities.

11. See Takahashi 1982 for a study of the Nisei generation's perceptions of race and race relations. This study does put a larger emphasis on white-Japanese relations than I do here.

12. In honesty, I must admit that I benefited from the students' struggles that spring. Their efforts were successful, and the Northwestern administration promised to begin the establishment of an Asian American studies program at Northwestern. As a result, the following fall I taught two Asian American studies courses. Northwestern University now has an Asian American studies program with two full-time faculty members.

3. Double-Crossing Chicago's Color Line

1. In fact I had had a difficult time finding an apartment to rent in my old "Scandinavian" neighborhood. I was attracted to the Far North Side neighborhood initially because of its low rents and its beautiful buildings. Andersonville was full of progressive homeowners and renters. It also was "liberal" enough to welcome the increasing numbers of same-sex couples, most of whom seemed to be white. I found it funny, though not shocking, that it did not seem to matter whom you slept with in Andersonville—as long as he or she was white.

2. Critiques, both negative and positive, of the Chicago School of Sociology and its legacy continue to be major topics among social scientists. Among these are Bulmer 1984, Fine 1995, Lindner 1996, and Plummer 1997.

3. The practice of studying one's own people may indeed be traceable to the research traditions and political dynamics present at the UCDS during its heyday. While the greatest number of "insider researchers" were black, the three Japanese Americans were clearly interpreting "Oriental culture" for their white colleagues and professors, just as the black researchers were providing insider information about blacks. I think it probable that this UCDS practice influences today's unspoken belief in the "native researcher" of color as the best interpreter of his or her group. Yu's study (2000) of Asian American scholars who studied and taught at UCDS provides a contemporary analysis and discussion of the Asian "insider researcher" at the University of Chicago.

4. The WRA poured funds into the relocation projects. In fact, part of the tension between Japanese Americans and blacks was due to the money and assistance that Japanese Americans were starting to receive as the war ended. Black leaders and some whites pointed this out to the relocatees more and more as Chicago's wartime economy experienced a mini-recession and times became harder for black Chicagoans.

5. Today Setsuko Matsunaga Nishi is professor emerita of sociology at Brooklyn College.

6. Okada finished his work in 1947, Uyeki in 1953, and Nishi in 1963. Although Okada's was the only research completed in the 1940s, all three projects were based on research that took place during or right after the arrival of Japanese Americans to Chicago.

7. With Daniel Patrick Moynihan suggesting that the black family was either pathological or at risk during this same time frame, Nishi's conclusions that it was Japanese Americans' families and culture that had saved them from poverty reflect the debates of the day. It could not have been coincidence that her study came out at the same time that "civil rights," "black power," and "war on poverty" were buzzwords.

8. Although contributors to Ong, Bonacich, and Cheng 1994 do not focus on the migration of Japanese and black labor to Chicago during the time frame that I discuss here, their focus on Asian migrant labor to the West Coast in the mid-nineties is similar in the types of questions and connections they make.

9. See Linehan 1993 for a study of how Japanese American resettlement in Cleveland affected and was affected by the city leaders' ideas of social engineering after World War II.

10. It seems that Chicago's brand of racism could be defined as "success as long as you know your place." Many of my informants voiced this sentiment in one way or the other: that you could be OK and make it as long as you knew your place. How this compared with blacks "staying in their place" is not clear. But it seems that both groups collectively stayed in their assigned places, which were of course lower than the ones that most whites occupied.

11. For an example, see Osako 1995.

12. One interesting account is found in Leonard 1992. Leonard tells of "Indians" (Sikh immigrants) in Brawlee, California, in the earlier part of this century drawing lines of demarcation between themselves, Mexicans, whites, and blacks. In this case, it seems that "black" was not at the bottom of the "coloreds" pile. Also of interest is Posadas's discussion (1994) of Filipino American households in Chicago since the early twentieth century. She argues that Filipino American identity was very much linked to the sexual relationships between Filipino men and white women in Chicago.

4. "Can You Imagine?"

1. Okihiro 1999 has a similar focus. Okihiro focuses on the letters and memories of Japanese American students during World War II. He argues that these accounts are important contributions in understanding the history of white antiracism activists in the United States.

2. See *Chicago Tribune Sunday Magazine,* November 5, 1990, for the article entitled "The New Geography." This feature includes numerous color photos and charts to accompany the Claritas Inc. research on Chicago neighborhoods and their classification by spending patterns. The article points out that the researchers are not "anthropologists, sociologists, or other social scientists from academia" but are marketing analysts interested in "modern American tribes."

3. Duis and La France 1992 and Osako 1995 both detail the resettlement patterns of Japanese Americans who relocated to Chicago during and right after World War II.

4. There is a growing body of research that is concerned with the global phenomenon of gentrification. One of the most thought-provoking of these studies is Smith 1996. Smith argues that cities in Europe, North America, and Australia have all experienced the same types of debilitating gentrification because of interconnected global political shifts.

5. The migration of poor whites from Appalachia (the "hillbillies" that Bill is referring to) to the Uptown neighborhood is an important part of the neighborhood's postwar history. Gitlin and Hollander 1970, Gitlin 1997, and Guy 1997 and 2000 are representative of the studies that focus on the complexities of southern white migrants and their interactions with their neighbors in the Far North Side of Chicago, Uptown in particular.

6. This part of Chicago's Far North Side has a long and interesting history of development. In 1891 the development of the area was called a "foolish and desperate enterprise" in a real-estate newspaper. In another strange twist, most of the Uptown buildings that are sought after today by rehabbers and urban pioneers were built by fast-buck landlords during the real estate boom of the 1920s and at the time were thought to be shabbily constructed. To complete the irony, this information appeared in an early 1990s edition of the *Chicago Rehabber* that encouraged the savvy rehabber to run, not walk, to Uptown for unbeatable opportunities.

7. The 100th/442nd fought in eight major campaigns in Italy, southern France, the Rhineland, and Central Europe from September 1943 to May 1945. See Duss 1987, Hawaii Nikkei History Editorial Board 1999, Matsuo and Hiura 1995, and Wakamatsu 1995 for further details on the experiences of Nisei soldiers during and after World War II.

8. On the unofficial 100th/442nd Web site (http://www.katonk.com/442nd.htm), the curator of the site tells a similar story that he heard from his mother about her cousin who went through basic training at Camp Shelby. That nameless cousin sent his family a letter that contained an interesting account of what happened when Nisei arrived in the southern United States. A group of Nisei soldiers saw a white man in a confrontation with a black woman on a crowded public bus. The soldiers allegedly forced the man and the driver off the bus and commandeered the bus, taking every person to his or her stop. The next day the soldiers were told by superiors that there had been complaints about Japanese soldiers beating up everyone on the bus, but their reprimand did not go beyond that. Regardless of the story's accuracy, such accounts exist. Certainly, Nisei soldiers posed a challenge to the daily operations of southern-style segregation.

9. The Stanley Park Hospital and Stanley Park community are pseudonyms.

10. Bill is talking about the better-known period of black inner-city rioting in the late 1960s. Yet Hirsch ([1983] 1995) believes that the race riots that took place in Chicago in the late 1940s were some of the worst in the country, although they are not part of popular conceptions of northern racial violence. The riots took place mostly on the South Side and began when whites acted in violent response to black families moving into public housing projects and private housing. Of these, the Cicero and Airport Homes riots in 1946, the Fernwood Riot of 1947, and the Englewood Riot in 1949 were the most notorious.

5. Give Me Five on the Black Man's Side

1. Hosokawa 1969 is a classic work that supports the notion that Japanese Americans, and Nisei in particular, are by nature conflict avoiders in American society. An alternative view of Japanese American activism can be found in another classic, Ichioka 1971.

2. Ichihashi (1932), a Japanese national, was concerned with the social problems that Japanese Americans faced in light of the economic and political changes on the West Coast. He had no idea that Internment would take place just ten years later, but it is interesting that he was predicting that Japanese Americans would undergo serious cultural changes because of American racism and discrimination.

3. During one of the monthly JACL Human Rights Committee meetings I attended, there was a discussion over the rape of a Japanese national female at a local college. Her accused attacker was a Japanese national male student. The incident had been brought to our attention by a Japanese lawyer who wanted support from the JACL. The committee members, all in their late sixties and seventies, spent some time arguing about the ways that "Japanese" men treated "Japanese" women, saying that this was America and the male perpetrator should pay for his crime.

4. The murder in the Palmer House shared Chicago's attention that weekend. The other story on the front pages of city newspapers was the murder of two white Chicago policemen by black snipers in the Cabrini-Green Housing Project.

5. Until recently Yuri Kochiyama's work with Malcolm X and her ongoing activism with the Puerto Rican nationalist movement in New York has garnered little attention. She has been arrested numerous times for civil disobedience. Yuri Kochiyama may be best known for the photo in which she is cradling Malcolm X's head right after he was fatally shot in Harlem in 1965.

6. During Internment there were two groups of Japanese Americans who resisted. About twelve thousand at Tule Lake were called the No-No Boys because of their answers to two loyalty questions asked of all interned Japanese Americans. The other group, eighty-five draft resisters at Heart Mountain, all served jail time, although they were eventually granted a presidential pardon by Harry Truman (see Mura 1993).

7. Vincent Chin was a Chinese American who was beaten to death by two unemployed white autoworkers in Detroit who "mistook" him for being Japanese. Neither of the two men ever served a day of jail time for the murder, although both were caught and admitted to committing the crime.

8. Kibbei are Japanese Americans who were born in the United States and then sent to Japan as children. They usually returned to the United States as young adults.

9. Thirteen days after the suit was filed, Mitsubishi gave 2,600 workers at the plant a day off with pay, free lunch, and transportation to Chicago so that they could rally in front of the EEOC offices in support of the company. The company also installed phones on the shop floor, so that employees could call their local and national representatives to protest the company's treatment.

10. I ignored the concerns of the group of ladies and later contacted the woman who had spoken up at the gathering. She sent me some of her materials and we made numerous dates for interviews, yet she always canceled them. After three cancellations, I decided that I would stop trying to contact her. This was a problem with two more women I attempted to interview early on in my fieldwork. Another Nisei woman, who spoke eloquently at the ceremony about her black husband and son, graciously agreed to be interviewed, but then called a few days later saying that she had changed her mind. Another Nisei woman, who lived in Heiwa Terrace, invited me up to her apartment after the ceremony. She offered me even more refreshments and invited me to come see her whenever I was in the building. Yet she, too, declined to be interviewed.

11. See Kendis 1989 for a different view of Nisei elderly. In Kendis's research, aging Nisei are kindly grandparents, not agitating activists. This is not to say that his research is inaccurate, but only to underscore the need for expanded understandings of expected and actual behavior of Nisei elders.

12. The fact that they were retired Japanese Americans who were in their seventies and eighties impressed me as well. During my fieldwork, I injured my knee. At one of our monthly Monday meetings, I limped into the JACL headquarters, and everyone showed sympathy. I was shocked at how much attention I was receiving, knowing that the members bundled themselves up against the Chicago weather and pulled themselves out of their homes to attend meetings and picket lines.

13. *Jet* magazine first reported in 1988 that Congressional Black Caucus Chairman Mervyn Dymally was "challenging" blacks to do what Japanese Americans had done. In the article, Dymally was quoted as saying, "It is not enough to be critical and say 'the Japanese got it, how come we can't get it?'" A year later *Jet* reported in "Reparation Bill for Blacks Pending in Congress" that Rep. John Conyers of Michigan had introduced legislation that would seek "$4 trillion in reparations for the descendants of African-American slaves." The most recent incarnation of the black reparations question came during a trip to Africa by President Bill Clinton in 1998, when he shocked many by apologizing (sort of) for slavery. But this controversial statement made it clear that monetary payments to the descendants of slaves was not an option.

Bibliography

Abelmann, Nancy, and John Lie. 1995. *Blue Dreams: Korean Americans and the Los Angeles Riots*. Cambridge: Harvard University Press.

Allen, Ernest, Jr. 1992. "When Japan Was 'Champion of the Darker Races': Satokata Takahashi and the Flowering of Black Messianic Nationalism." *Black Scholar* 24 (1): 23–46.

Andersonville Chamber of Commerce. 1996. *A Walk through Andersonville*.

Barrett, Paul M. 1999. *The Good Black: A True Story of Race in America*. New York: Dutton.

Bell, Bernard W., Emily Grosholz, and James B. Stewart, eds. 1998. *W. E. B. Du Bois on Race and Culture: Philosophy, Politics, and Poetics*. New York: Routledge.

Berlant, Lauren. 1997. *The Queen of America Goes to Washington City: Essays on Sex and Citizenship*. Durham: Duke University Press.

Broom, Leonard, and John I. Kitsuse. 1973. *The Managed Casualty: The Japanese-American Family in World War II*. Berkeley and Los Angeles: University of California Press.

Buckley, William F., Jr. 1997. "Drumming Up Ethnic Hurt." On-line column, http://www.uexpress.com/ups/opinion/column/wb/text/1997/03/wb970325.html. Accessed March 27, 1997.

Bulmer, Martin. 1984. *The Chicago School of Sociology*. Chicago: University of Chicago Press.

Caudill, William A., and George DeVos. 1956. "Achievement, Culture, and Personality: The Case of the Japanese-Americans." *American Anthropologist* 58: 1102–26.

Chang, Edward T., and Russell C. Leong, eds. 1993. *Los Angeles—Struggles toward Multiethnic Community: Asian American, African American, and Latino Perspectives*. Seattle: University of Washington Press.

Chicago Resettlers' Committee (CRC). 1946. *Sociological Report of the Special Analysis Committee*. Chicago Historical Society, Miscellaneous Pamphlets of the Chicago Resettlers' Committee.

———. 1947. *Chicago Resettlement 1947: A Report.* Chicago Historical Society, Miscellaneous Pamphlets of the Chicago Resettlers' Committee.

City of Chicago Department of Planning and Development. 1992. *Social and Economic Characteristics of Chicago's Population.* 1990 Census of Population and Housing—Report no. 2. Chicago.

Cohen, Lawrence. 1994. "Old Age: Cultural and Critical Perspectives." *Annual Review of Anthropology* 23: 137–58.

Daniels, Roger. 1978. *The Politics of Prejudice: The Anti-Japanese Movement in California and the Struggle for Japanese Exclusion.* Berkeley and Los Angeles: University of California Press.

di Leonardo, Micaela. 1998. *Exotics at Home: Anthropologies, Others, American Modernity.* Chicago: University of Chicago Press.

Drake, St. Clair, and Horace R. Cayton. [1945] 1993. *Black Metropolis: A Study of Negro Life in a Northern City.* Reprint, with a foreword by William Julius Wilson, Chicago: University of Chicago Press.

Du Bois, W. E. B. 1906. "The Colorline Belts the World." In *W. E. B. Du Bois: A Reader,* edited by David Levering Lewis. New York: Holt.

———. 1915. "The Negro Problems." In *W. E. B. Du Bois: A Reader,* edited by David Levering Lewis. New York: Holt.

Duis, Perry, and Scott La France. 1992. *We've Got a Job to Do: Chicagoans and World War II.* Chicago: Chicago Historical Society.

Duss, Masayo Umezawa. 1987. *Unlikely Liberators: The Men of the 100th and 442nd.* Honolulu: University of Hawaii Press.

Fine, Gary A., ed. 1995. *A Second Chicago School: The Development of a Post-War American Sociology.* Chicago: University of Chicago Press.

Frazier, E. Franklin. 1932. *The Negro Family in Chicago.* Chicago: University of Chicago Press.

Gallicchio, Marc. 2000. *The African American Encounter with Japan and China.* Chapel Hill: University of North Carolina Press.

Gehrie, Mark Joshua. 1973. "Sansei: An Ethnography of Experience." Ph.D. diss., Northwestern University.

Gitlin, Todd. 1997. "Organizing across Boundaries: Beyond Identity Politics." *Dissent* 44: 38–40.

Gitlin, Todd, and Nanci Hollander. 1970. *Uptown: Poor Whites in Chicago.* New York: Harper and Row.

Glazer, Nathan, ed. 1970. *Cities in Trouble.* Chicago: Quadrangle Books.

Glenn, Evelyn Nakano. 1988. *Issei, Nisei, War Bride: Three Generations of Japanese American Women in Domestic Service.* Philadelphia: Temple University Press.

Goldfield, Michael. 1997. *The Color of Politics: Race and the Mainsprings of American Politics.* New York: New Press.

Gooding-Williams, Robert, ed. 1993. *Reading Rodney King/Reading Urban Uprising.* New York: Routledge.

Greenberg, Cheryl. 1995. "Black and Jewish Responses to Japanese Internment." *Journal of American Ethnic History* 14 (2): 4–37.

Guy, Roger Stephen. 1997. "Down Home: Perception and Reality among Southern White Migrants in Post World War II Chicago." *Oral History Review* 24 (2): 35–53.

————. 2000. "The Media, the Police, and Southern White Migrant Identity in Chicago, 1955–1970." *Journal of Urban History* 26 (3): 329–49.

Harden, Jacalyn D. 1997. "The Enterprise of Empire: Race, Class, Gender, and Japanese National Identity." In *The Gender Sexuality Reader,* edited by Roger N. Lancaster and Micaela di Leonardo. New York: Routledge.

Harris, Neil. 1990. "All the World a Melting Pot? Japan at American Fairs, 1876–1904." In *Cultural Excursions: Marketing Appetites and Tastes in Modern America.* Chicago: University of Chicago Press.

Harrison, Faye V. 1988. "Introduction: An African Diaspora Perspective for Urban Anthropology." *Urban Anthropology* 17 (2–3): 111–20.

————. 1995. "The Persistent Power of 'Race' in the Cultural and Political Economy of Racism." *Annual Review of Anthropology* 24: 47–74.

Hatamiya, Leslie T. 1993. *Righting a Wrong: Japanese Americans and the Passage of the Civil Liberties Act of 1988.* Stanford: Stanford University Press.

Hawaii Nikkei History Editorial Board, ed. 1999. *Japanese Eyes, American Hearts: Personal Reflections of Hawaii's World War II Nisei Soldiers.* Honolulu: University of Hawaii Press.

Hellwig, David J. 1977. "Afro-American Reactions to the Japanese and Anti-Japanese Movement, 1906–1924." *Phylon* 38 (1): 93–104.

Hirsch, Arnold R. [1983] 1995. *Making the Second Ghetto: Race and Housing in Chicago, 1940–1960.* Reprint, Cambridge: Cambridge University Press.

Hirsch, Eric L. 1990. *Urban Revolt: Ethnic Politics in the Nineteenth-Century Chicago Labor Movement.* Berkeley and Los Angeles: University of California Press.

Holli, Melvin G., and Peter d'A. Jones., eds. 1997. *Ethnic Chicago: A Multicultural Portrait.* 2nd ed. Grand Rapids, Mich.: Eerdmans.

Hosokawa, Bill. 1969. *Nisei: The Quiet Americans.* New York: Morrow.

————. 1982. *JACL in Quest of Justice: The History of the Japanese American Citizens League.* New York: Morrow.

Houri, William. 1988. *Repairing America: An Account of the Movement for Japanese-American Redress.* Pullman: Washington State University Press.

Ichihashi, Yamato. 1932. *Japanese in the United States: A Critical Study of the Problems of the Japanese Immigrants and Their Children.* Stanford: Stanford University Press.

Ichioka, Yuji. 1971. "A Buried Past: Early Issei Socialists and the Japanese Community." *Amerasia Journal* 1 (2): 1–25.

Irwin, Wallace. 1921. *Seed of the Sun.* New York: Doravan.

Jaimes, M. Annette, ed. 1992. *The State of Native America: Genocide, Colonization, and Resistance.* Boston: South End Press.

Katz, Michael B., and Thomas J. Sugrue, eds. 1998. *W. E. B. Du Bois, Race, and the City: The Philadelphia Negro and Its Legacy.* Philadelphia: University of Pennsylvania Press.

Kearney, Reginald. 1991. "Afro-American Views of the Japanese, 1900–1945." Ph.D. diss., Kent State University.

Kendis, Randall Jay. 1989. *An Attitude of Gratitude: The Adaptation to Aging of the Elderly Japanese in America.* New York: AMS Press.

Kim, Claire. 2000. *Bitter Fruit: The Politics of Black-Korean Conflict in New York City.* New Haven: Yale University Press.

Kim, Elaine H., Eui-Young Yu, and Anna Deavere Smith. 1997. *East to America: Korean American Life Stories*. New York: New Press.

Kim, Kwang Chung, ed. 1999. *Koreans in the Hood*. Baltimore: Johns Hopkins University Press.

Kristol, Irving. 1970. "The Negro Today Is Like the Immigrant Yesterday." In *Cities in Trouble*, edited by Nathan Glazer (Chicago: Quadrangle Books). First published in *New York Times Magazine*, September 11, 1966.

Kyne, Peter B. 1935. *The Pride of Palomar*. In *The Peter B. Kyne Omnibus*. New York: Grosset and Dunlap.

Lait, Jack, and Lee Mortimer. 1950. *Chicago Confidential*. New York: Crown.

Lee, Robert G. 1999. *Orientals: Asian Americans in Popular Culture*. Philadelphia: Temple University Press.

Leonard, Karen Isaksen. 1992. *Making Ethnic Choices: California's Punjabi Mexican Americans*. Philadelphia: Temple University Press.

Lindner, Rolf. 1996. *The Reportage of Urban Culture: Robert Park and the Chicago School*. Cambridge: Cambridge University Press.

Linehan, Thomas M. 1993. "Japanese American Resettlement in Cleveland during and after World War II." *Journal of Urban History* 20 (1): 54–80.

Liss, Julia E. 1998. "Diasporic Identities: The Science and Politics of Race in the Work of Franz Boas and W. E. B. Du Bois, 1894–1919." *Cultural Anthropology* 13 (2): 127–66.

Loewen, James W. 1999. *The Mississippi Chinese: Between Black and White*. 2nd ed. Prospect Heights, Ill.: Waveland Press.

Lowe, Lisa. 1996. *Immigrant Acts: On Asian American Cultural Politics*. Durham: Duke University Press.

Lutz, Catherine A., and Jane L. Collins. 1993. *Reading National Geographic*. Chicago: University of Chicago Press.

Marcus, George E. 1998. *Ethnography through Thick and Thin*. Princeton: Princeton University Press.

Matsumoto, Valerie J. 1993. *Farming the Home Place: A Japanese American Community in California, 1919–1982*. Ithaca: Cornell University Press.

Matsuo, Dorothy, and Arnold Hiura, eds. 1995. *Boyhood to War: History and Anecdotes of the 442nd Regimental Combat Team*. Honolulu: Mutual.

Min, Pyong Gap. 1996. *Caught in the Middle: Korean Merchants in America's Multiethnic Cities*. Berkeley and Los Angeles: University of California Press.

Miyagawa, Dyke. 1949. "Africa Was Never Like That!" *Scene: The Pictorial Magazine*, November, 14–17.

Motzafi-Haller, Pnina. 1997. "Writing Birthright: On Native Anthropologists and the Politics of Representation." In *Auto/Ethnography*, edited by Deborah E. Reed-Danahay. New York: Berg.

Mukhopadhyay, Carol, and Yolanda Moses. 1997. "Reestablishing Race in Anthropological Discourse." *American Anthropologist* 99 (3): 517–33.

Mura, David. 1993. "No-No Boys: Re-X-Amining Japanese Americans." *New England Review* 15 (3): 143–65.

Nishi, Setsuko Matsunaga. 1963. "Japanese American Achievement in Chicago: A Cultural Response to Degradation." Ph.D. diss., University of Chicago.

O'Brien, David J., and Stephen S. Fugita. 1991. *The Japanese American Experience*. Bloomington: Indiana University Press.

Okada, Dave. 1947. "Two Chicago Industrial Plants under Wartime Conditions." Ph.D. diss., University of Chicago.

Okihiro, Gary. 1994. *Margins and Mainstreams: Asians in American History and Culture.* Seattle: University of Washington Press.

————. 1999. *Storied Lives: Japanese American Students and World War II.* Seattle: University of Washington Press.

Omatsu, Glenn. 1994. "The 'Four Prisons' and the Movements of Liberation: Asian American Activism from the 1960s to the 1990s." In *The State of Asian America: Activism and Resistance in the 1990s,* edited by Karin Aguilar-San Juan. Boston: South End Press.

Omi, Michael, and Howard Winant. 1994. *Racial Formation in the United States: From the 1960s to the 1990s.* New York: Routledge.

Ong, Paul, Edna Bonacich, and Lucie Cheng, eds. 1994. *The New Asian Immigration in Los Angeles and Global Restructuring.* Philadelphia: Temple University Press.

Osako, Masaoka. 1995. "Japanese Americans: Melting into the All-American Melting Pot." In *Ethnic Chicago: A Multicultural Portrait,* edited by Melvin G. Holli and Peter d'A. Jones. Grand Rapids, Mich.: Eerdmans.

Park, Kyeyoung. 1995. "The Re-Invention of Affirmative Action: Changing Conceptions of African Americans and Latin Americans." *Urban Anthropology* 24 (1–2): 59–92.

————. 1996. "Use and Abuse of Race and Culture: Black-Korean Tension in America." *American Anthropologist* 98 (3): 492–99.

————. 1997. *The Korean American Dream: Immigrants and Small Business in New York City.* Ithaca: Cornell University Press.

Park, Robert E. 1950. *Race and Culture.* New York: Free Press.

Petersen, William. 1970. "Success Story, Japanese-American Style." In *Cities in Trouble,* edited by Nathan Glazer (Chicago: Quadrangle Books). First published in *New York Times Magazine,* January 9, 1966.

Plummer, Ken., ed. 1997. *Chicago School.* New York: Routledge.

Posadas, Barbara M. 1994. "Crossed Boundaries in Interracial Chicago: Filipino American Families since 1925." In *Unequal Sisters: A Multi-Cultural Reader in U.S. Women's History,* edited by Vicki L. Ruiz and Carol DuBois, 316–29. New York: Routledge.

Prashad, Vijay. 1998. "Anti-D'Souza: The Ends of Racism and the Asian American." *Amerasia Journal* 24 (1): 23–40.

————. 2000. *The Karma of Brown Folk.* Minneapolis: University of Minnesota Press.

————. 2001. *Everybody Was Kung Fu Fighting: Afro-Asian Connections and the Myth of Cultural Purity.* Boston: Beacon Press.

"The Race War That Flopped." 1946. *Ebony,* July, 3–9.

Raybon, Patricia. 1997. *My First White Friend: Confessions on Race, Love, Forgiveness.* New York: Penguin.

Reed, Adolph, Jr. 1997. *W. E. B. Du Bois and American Political Thought: Fabianism and the Color Line.* Oxford: Oxford University Press.

"Reparation Bill for Blacks Pending in Congress." 1989. *Jet,* December 25, 10.

Roediger, David. 1991. *The Wages of Whiteness: Race and the Making of the American Working Class.* New York: Verso.

Rydell, Robert W. 1984. *All the World's a Fair: Visions of Empire at American International Expositions, 1876–1916.* Chicago: University of Chicago Press.

Sakai, J. 1983. *Settlers: The Mythology of the White Proletariat.* Chicago: Morningstar Press.

"Seattle's Little Big-Leaguers." 1953. *Scene: The Pictorial Magazine,* February, 25–27.

Shankman, Arnold. 1982. *Ambivalent Friends: Afro-Americans View the Immigrant.* Contributions in Afro-American and African Studies, no. 6. Westport, Conn.: Greenwood.

Shipler, David K. 1997. *A Country of Strangers.* New York: Knopf.

Sleeper, Jim. 1997. *Liberal Racism.* New York: Viking.

Smith, Neil. 1996. *The New Urban Frontier: Gentrification and the Revanchist City.* New York: Routledge.

Spickard, Paul R. 1983. "The Nisei Assume Power: The Japanese American Citizens League, 1941–1942." *Pacific Historical Review* 52: 147–74.

———. 1996. *Japanese Americans: The Formation and Transformations of an Ethnic Group.* New York: Twayne.

State of California Department of Justice. 1946. *Police Training Bulletin: A Guide to Race Relations for Police Officers,* by Davis McEntire and Robert B. Powers.

Steinhorn, Leonard, and Barbara Diggs-Brown. 1999. *By the Color of Our Skin.* New York: Dutton.

Storn, Orin. 1986. "Engineering Internment: Anthropologists and the War Relocation Authority." *American Ethnologist* 13: 700–720.

Sumida, Stephen H. 1998. "East of California: Points of Origin in Asian American Studies." *Journal of Asian American Studies* 1 (1): 83–100.

Takahashi, Jere. 1982. "Japanese American Responses to Race Relations: The Formation of Nisei Perspectives." *Amerasia Journal* 9 (1): 29–57.

Takaki, Ronald T. 1990. *Iron Cages: Race and Culture in Nineteenth-Century America.* New York: Oxford University Press.

Takezawa, Yasuko I. 1995. *Breaking the Silence: Redress and Japanese American Ethnicity.* Ithaca: Cornell University Press.

Tamura, Linda. 1994. *The Hood River Issei.* Urbana: University of Illinois Press.

Taylor, Quintard. 1998. *In Search of America's New Racial Frontier: African Americans in the American West, 1528–1990.* New York: Norton.

Thernstrom, Stephan, and Abigail M. Thernstrom. 1997. *America in Black and White: One Nation Indivisible.* New York: Simon and Schuster.

Thomas, Dorothy S., Charles Kikuchi, and James Sakoda. 1952. *The Salvage.* Berkeley and Los Angeles: University of California Press.

U.S. War Relocation Authority (WRA). 1945. *Speaker's Guide on Relocation in Chicago,* by W. W. Lessing. Chicago.

Uyeki, Eugene S. 1953. "Process and Patterns of Nisei Adjustment to Chicago." Ph.D. diss., University of Chicago.

Visweswaran, Kamala. 1998. "Race and the Culture of Anthropology." *American Anthropologist* 100 (1): 70–83.

Wakamatsu, Jack K. 1995. *Silent Warriors: A Memoir of America's 442nd Regimental Combat Team.* New York: Vantage.

Wang, L. Ling-chi. 1998. "Race, Class, Citizenship, and Extraterritoriality: Asian Americans and the 1996 Campaign Finance Scandal." *Amerasia Journal* 24 (1): 1–21.

Weglyn, Michi. 1976. *Years of Infamy: The Untold Story of America's Concentration Camps.* New York: Morrow Press.

Williams, Brett. 1988. *Upscaling Downtown: Stalled Gentrification in Washington, D.C.* Ithaca: Cornell University Press.

Wu, Frank H. 2001. *Yellow: Race in America beyond Black and White.* New York: Basic Books.

Yanagisako, Sylvia Junko. 1992. *Transforming the Past: Tradition and Kinship among Japanese Americans.* Stanford: Stanford University Press.

Yoon, In-Jin. 1997. *On My Own: Korean Immigration, Entrepreneurship, and Korean-Black Relations in Chicago and Los Angeles.* Chicago: University of Chicago Press.

Yu, Henry. 2000. *Thinking Orientals: Migration, Contact, and Exoticism in Modern America.* New York: Oxford University Press.

Index

Jacalyn D. Harden is assistant professor of anthropology in the Department of Society, Justice, and Culture at Seattle University. Her current project studies race and technological change at the beginning of the twenty-first century.